# THE NSA SUPPORTS
## THE ADVANCEMENT OF UNIQUE AND DIVERSE WOMEN.

**SWE Magazine's 2022 State of Women in Engineering edition is sponsored by the National Security Agency.**

MAGAZINE OF THE SOCIETY OF WOMEN ENGINEERS

Society of Women Engineers
130 E. Randolph Street, Suite 3500
Chicago, Illinois 60601
Phone: 877.793.4636
Fax: 312.596.5252
Website: www.swe.org
Email: hq@swe.org

VOLUME 68 | NUMBER 2 | STATE OF WOMEN IN ENGINEERING 2022

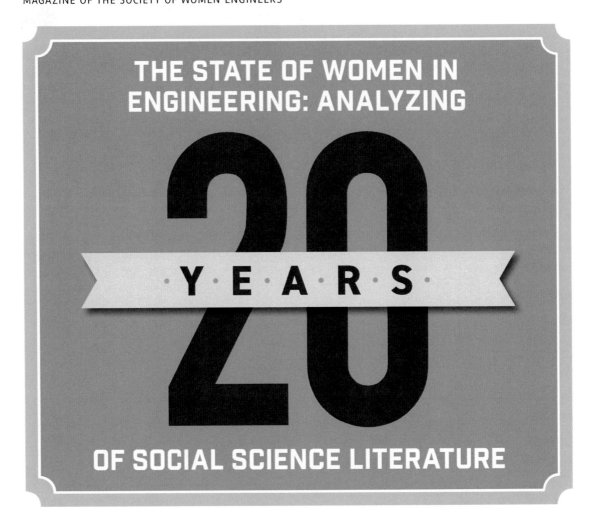

THE STATE OF WOMEN IN ENGINEERING: ANALYZING 20 YEARS OF SOCIAL SCIENCE LITERATURE

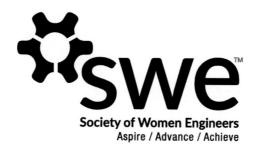

## Engage with *SWE Magazine* articles

apexawards.com

**EDITORIAL:**
Anne M. Perusek
Director of Editorial
and Publications
anne.perusek@swe.org

Carol Polakowski
Senior Editor
carol.polakowski@swe.org

JoAnn Dickey Design
Art Direction and Production

**RESEARCH:**
Roberta Rincon, Ph.D.
SWE Associate Director of
Research
roberta.rincon@swe.org

**ABOUT SWE:**
The Society of Women Engineers (SWE), founded in 1950, is a not-for-profit educational and service organization. SWE is the driving force that establishes engineering as a highly desirable career aspiration for women. SWE empowers women to succeed and advance in those aspirations and be recognized for their life-changing contributions and achievements as women engineers and leaders.

SWE (ISSN 1070-6232), Magazine of the Society of Women Engineers, is published quarterly by the Society of Women Engineers, 130 East Randolph Street, Suite 3500, Chicago, Illinois 60601.

**ADVERTISING RATES:**
For advertising rates and information, contact SWE's business development manager: Monica.Mizzi@swe.org

**ANNUAL SUBSCRIPTION RATES:**
SWE members, $10.00 included in dues; SWE student members, $7.50 included in dues; non-members, $30.00. Periodicals postage paid at Chicago, IL and additional mailing offices.

**POSTMASTER:**
Send address changes to: SWE, c/o Society of Women Engineers at the above address.

© Copyright 2022 Society of Women Engineers

# RESEARCH AND TRENDS
## FOR WOMEN IN STEM

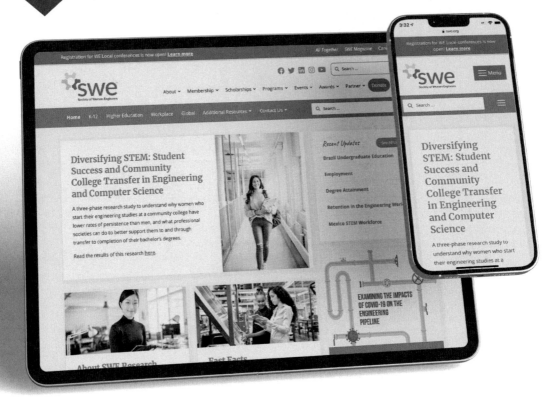

Let SWE's research site be your #1 resource for the latest studies and stats on the state of women in engineering.

**LEARN MORE ABOUT:**

| SWE RESEARCH AND CONTACTS | HIGHER EDUCATION | WORKPLACE | K-12 | GLOBAL |
|---|---|---|---|---|

# A 20-Year Retrospective

RECOGNIZING THE VALUE OF RESEARCH AND ITS ACCOMPANYING PUBLIC POLICY IMPLICATIONS, WHAT BEGAN AS A SINGLE, LENGTHY ARTICLE GREW TO BECOME, IN 2017, OUR ANNUAL STATE OF WOMEN IN ENGINEERING ISSUE, AND A SESSION OF THE SAME NAME AT THE SWE ANNUAL CONFERENCE.

At a brainstorming session more than 20 years ago, the concept for SWE's annual review of social science literature on women in engineering took shape. We closed the *SWE Magazine* editorial board meeting that day with plans to publish our review the following spring. And in the April/May 2002 issue, we launched the first of what has become more than two decades of literature reviews — discussions of the previous year's research themes and findings, alongside an extensive bibliography.

Over time, our reviews expanded to include interesting, in-depth sidebar material, and as it became available, more research from outside the United States. At this writing, the compilation of our literature reviews consists of nearly 500 pages. Updated annually, it can be found on SWE's research site: https://swe.org/research/.

The original intention behind the reviews has remained the same, however. By examining what peer-reviewed social science research tells us, we can take appropriate and effective steps toward solving the puzzle of the persistent underrepresentation of women in engineering.

Recognizing the value of research and its accompanying public policy implications, what began as a single, lengthy article grew to become, in 2017, our annual State of Women in Engineering issue, and a session of the same name at the SWE annual conference. The literature review is the backbone of the State of Women in Engineering issue, with additional articles on SWE's own research and policy efforts, and examinations of myriad related issues.

Lead author of the literature review, Peter Meiksins, Ph.D., has been part of the literature review team for more than half of the 20 years we are celebrating in this issue. A sociologist and now professor emeritus, Dr. Meiksins' grasp of the research themes, methodologies, and findings has resulted in highly readable, cogent discussions and insights. Taking on the challenge of analyzing the past 20 years of our reviews, while bringing the most relevant research from 2021 into the discussion, he has provided a valuable service. Dr. Meiksins addresses, for example, how some early explanations regarding the underrepresentation of women have proved unfounded. And while there are areas of consensus, other explanations remain topics for debate, yet newer research questions provide fresh tools from which to problem-solve.

Understanding what has been learned over the past two decades, what questions remain unanswered, what has changed, what has not, and the policy implications stemming from these realities are key to moving forward. We hope you will join us in this endeavor.

*Anne M. Perusek*

*Director of Editorial & Publications*
*anne.perusek@swe.org*

# Women in Engineering: Analyzing 20 Years of Social Science Literature

For the past two decades, SWE has conducted an annual review of the social science research addressing the underrepresentation of women in engineering. This retrospective examines what has been learned in that time, what questions remain unanswered, what has changed, what has not, and the policy implications stemming from these realities.

By Peter Meiksins, Ph.D., Cleveland State University
   Peggy Layne, P.E., F.SWE, Virginia Tech

In 2001, SWE initiated its annual review of the research literature on women in engineering with a view to making women engineers in industry, the public sector, and the academy more aware of the findings of social science research on the experiences of women engineers and the reasons for the relatively small numbers of women entering the profession. For the past 20 years, the review has appeared in the pages of *SWE Magazine*, reporting on the growing body of research published each year. Since 2021 marks 20 years of literature reviews, it seems appropriate to look back over previous reviews to try to determine what has been learned and what questions remain unanswered. This retrospective review will also provide an opportunity to assess to what extent and how the situation of women in engineering has changed. Such an assessment will help shed light on whether the many policy changes and innovative programs described in previous years' research have borne fruit and whether changes "on the ground" have led researchers to shift their focus in response to new realities.

We begin our retrospective look at research on women in engineering with a review of the empirical situation. Has there been progress in increasing the numbers of women in engineering and, if so, how much and in what areas? We then review the main themes on which research has focused over the past two decades, indicating both shifts in research emphasis and ongoing themes that have been central all along. Throughout that review, we will summarize research published in 2021 that made significant contributions to what we know.

Finally, we conclude with comments on what a retrospective look at the research literature teaches us about what would be needed to accelerate progress toward gender equity in engineering.

## A REVIEW OF THE NUMBERS — HOW MUCH CHANGE HAS THERE BEEN?

Reviewing the situation in the early 2020s, one feels a mixture of encouragement that women have become a much more significant presence in engineering in the past few decades and disappointment that the field has not become fully gender-balanced, despite decades of research examining the reasons for gender imbalances, numerous programs designed to attract more girls to engineering, well-funded national programs such as NSF-ADVANCE, and the efforts of important national organizations, including the American Association of University Women and SWE. As the statistical data presented here show, while there has been progress, it has been slow in the 21st century, and women still represent a minority of both engineering students, faculty, and employed engineers more broadly.

One must be careful in interpreting data on the share of the profession occupied by men and women. As previous literature review author Lisa Frehill long ago pointed out, the increase in the percentage of engineering students who were women in the last few decades of the 20th century was as much a function of the *decline* in male enrollment as anything else — women were not more likely to enroll in engineering programs in 2001 than they had been 15 years earlier.[i] As engineering enrollments have grown in the last decade or two, there has been increasing interest in engineering among male students, meaning that women's enrollment would have had to grow even faster for their share of engineering degrees to increase.

That said, the data presented here document real change. First, it is obvious that there has been a significant increase in the share of engineering degrees at all levels going to women. For example, women earned less than 1% of engineering B.S. degrees in 1954; that share had increased to 23% in 2020. Similarly impressive increases occurred for master's and doctoral degrees in the same period. A bit less encouragingly, however, the most significant increases occurred in the 1970s and 1980s; since 1990, women's share of engineering degrees has grown, but much more slowly. If trends continue, it will take decades for anything close to gender parity in degree attainment to be achieved.

The percentage of engineering degrees going to women varies by discipline; in 2020, women earned fully half of bachelor's degrees in biomedical engineering, but only 16.5% of bachelor's degrees in mechanical engineering. Notably, women's share of bachelor's degrees by discipline has been quite stable over the past 20 years. For example, women earned 37% of bachelor's degrees in chemical engineering in 2002 and 37.7% in 2020; in mechanical engineering, the percentages were 14% in 2002 and 16.5% in 2020.

The share of engineering degrees earned by women varies by race and ethnicity, although not enormously. Among African Americans and Asian Americans, women's share of bachelor's degrees in engineering was somewhat higher (closer to 30%), while it was lower for other groups. It should be added that the number of engineering degrees earned by African Americans of either sex was quite small, so one should not exaggerate the significance of the higher percentage earned by African American women.

Data on faculty reveal a pattern similar to that for students. Overall, the share of faculty positions in engineering held by women doubled between

continued on page 10

## Engineering Bachelor's Degrees by Gender within Race/Ethnicity, 2020

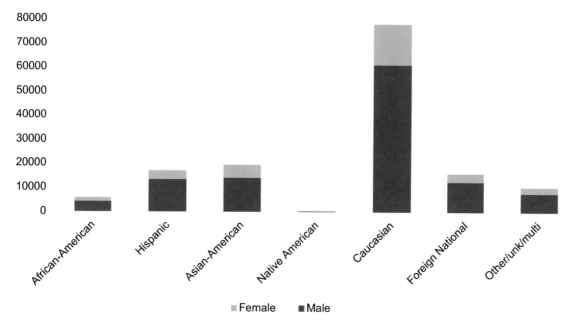

Female   Male

(Source: ASEE (2021) Profiles of Engineering and Engineering Technology. Washington DC)

# Artificial Intelligence, Inequality, and Power

Over the past several years, news media, including *SWE Magazine*, have reported on a series of controversies involving technology companies and the development and use of artificial intelligence (AI). Among the more important controversies were organized employee protests against the involvement of tech companies in assisting the military as well as immigration authorities with AI. Criticisms have also been levied against AI technologies that incorporate racial, gender, and other forms of bias. Technology companies have tried to respond by developing ethical codes regarding AI and its uses, but the tensions have not been eliminated. For example, last year, *SWE Magazine* (2021) reported on the departure of a leading member of Google's AI ethics team, Timnit Gebru, Ph.D. Although Google denied it, Dr. Gebru claimed that she was fired because of her desire to publish a paper on how AI mimics language that could hurt marginalized groups. This year, another Google AI ethics researcher, Margaret Mitchell, Ph.D., was fired by Google for what the company said were violations of the company's code of conduct and security protocols. But, Mitchell claims that it was actually her critique of the company's AI work that motivated her termination (The Guardian 2021).

The controversy over AI, gender, diversity, and ethics is placed in a much broader context by *The Atlas of AI*, a book published by prominent AI researcher, Kate Crawford, Ph.D. (2021). Dr. Crawford is research professor of communication and science and technology studies at the University of Southern California and a senior principal researcher at Microsoft Research. She also served as the inaugural visiting chair for AI and justice at the École normale supérieure in Paris.

## MORE THAN JUST A BUG TO BE FIXED

Dr. Crawford describes how much of the contemporary criticism of AI focuses on concerns that it contains built-in social biases, so that its use reproduces or even intensifies the unequal treatment of disadvantaged groups. She shows, in her book, that these biases derive of the way AI "learns." Typically, AI systems are developed through the use of test data harvested from publicly available online sources. These data sets generally are not fully representative of the overall population; indeed, they often are skewed, include biased language, or contain gaps that omit whole groups of people or aspects of human experience. Making matters worse, these data then need to be classified, which requires the development of a classification system, which is another vector through which bias can enter the system (the classification system itself can be biased) and a huge amount of manual labor to sort the data into the classification system employed. More often than not, this work is performed by poorly paid, crowdsourced labor obtained through portals such as Amazon's Mechanical Turk, which means both that the work of classifying involves a hidden form of exploitation and that it is vulnerable to inaccuracies as workers hurry to complete the "piecework" tasks they have taken on. Finally, since newer AI systems often build on the ones that came before, biases incorporated in early systems tend to become parts of subsequent technologies. Users are often unaware of these biases in the systems they employ.

According to Dr. Crawford, "the AI industry has traditionally understood the problem of bias as though it is a bug to be fixed..." (130). Recent corporate attempts to deal with the problem of bias in AI used in hiring illustrate this approach well. Many organizations use AI to screen resumés, but the technology involved has been criticized for unintentionally incorporating a range of racial, gender, and other biases. Dr. Crawford, for example, notes how Amazon developed an AI-based hiring system that rarely recommended female candidates, largely because the system "learned" using data from previous searches that had hired mostly men. Awareness of this problem has led to efforts to detect bias in AI and find ways to eliminate it. *The New York Times* recently reported (Lohr 2021) that a group of major corporations (including CVS Health, Deloitte, GM, Humana, IBM, Mastercard, Meta, Nike, and Walmart) has partnered with the Data and Trust Alliance, an organization that has developed an evaluation and scoring system for AI software. The hope is that using this system will allow employers to detect bias in their AI systems so that they can combat it and develop more effective AI tools for evaluating job applications.

Dr. Crawford sees steps such as this one as largely positive, but she feels the problems go deeper. She contends that:

"AI systems are not autonomous, rational, or able to discern anything without extensive computationally intensive training with large data sets or predefined rules and rewards. In fact, artificial intelligence as we know it depends entirely on a much wider set of political and social structures. And due to the capital required to build AI at scale and the ways of seeing that it optimizes, AI systems are ultimately designed to serve existing dominant interests. In this sense artificial intelligence is a registry of power" (8).

## AI'S CONSTRUCTION OF RACE AND GENDER

She argues that AI inevitably involves classification, imposing a set of predetermined categories on a complex reality, making it effectively an exercise of power. Any classification system involves a socially influenced oversimplification of reality, or, as Dr. Crawford puts it: "Machine learning systems are, in a very real way, *constructing* race and gender: they are defining the world within the terms they have set, and this has long-lasting ramifications for the people who are classified" (146). Dr. Crawford expresses concern about how AI has increasingly been used in ways that affect ordinary people in civilian life: in support of law enforcement, in hiring processes, even in attempting to detect ineligible welfare recipients and unemployment insurance abuse.

In her view, AI embodies power in another sense. Those with the resources to obtain the training data on which AI learning depends, to organize the labor of classification and checking it requires, and to build and deploy these complex technological systems, tend to be large organizations: governments, corporations, and the like. The "object" of AI, i.e., ordinary people, generally do not know they are part of the training data, nor are they consulted or given an opportunity to influence the classification systems AI employs. When those systems are proprietary, as is the case for some of the most powerful, ubiquitous ones (Google, Facebook, etc.), it is even less likely that they will be subject to the scrutiny of anyone other than the systems' owners.

So, while Dr. Crawford agrees that AI systems can and should be examined to expose the biases they may embody, she feels that a wider range of voices needs to be included in that examination so that those *affected* by the work of AI systems can be heard (Corbyn 2021).

Kate Crawford, research professor of communication and science and technology studies, USC; senior principal researcher, Microsoft Research; and author of *Atlas of AI*.

She also emphasizes that it is not enough just to apply technical fixes to existing AI systems; the power structure those systems serve needs to be understood and problematized. Finally, she calls for a "renewed politics of refusal" (Corbyn 2021), for a willingness to say that not all AI systems are beneficial or needed: "Rather than asking where AI will be applied, merely because it can, the emphasis should be on *why* it ought to be applied" (226).

### References

Corbyn, Z. (2021). Interview: Microsoft's Kate Crawford: "AI Is Neither Artificial Nor Intelligent." The Observer. June 6.

Crawford, K. (2021). The Atlas of AI: Power, Politics and the Planetary Costs of Artificial Intelligence. *New Haven, Conn: Yale University Press.*

Lohr, S. (2021). Group Backed by Top Companies Moves to Combat A.I. Bias in Hiring. The New York Times, *Dec. 8.*

SWE Magazine (2021). Gender Equity and Social Justice at Uber and Google. State of Women in Engineering 2021: 40–42.

The Guardian (2021). Google Fires Margaret Mitchell, Another Top Researcher on Its AI Team. Feb 19.

*continued from page 7*

2002 and 2021, from 9.25% to 18.5%. This is an impressive increase, although women still represent a distinct minority of engineering faculty. The pattern of doubling is apparent for most disciplines within engineering, although it remains the case that certain disciplines are less "female" than others — e.g., mechanical and electrical engineering have smaller percentages of female faculty (in the 15% range), while chemical, civil, and biomedical engineering are higher (over 20%). The percentage of faculty who are female decreases with rank: In 2020, only 13.6% of full professors of engineering were women, compared with 25.4% of assistant professors. In one sense, this represents a perpetuation of the situation that prevailed 20 years earlier — in 2002, 4.7% of engineering full professors were women, compared with 17% of assistant professors. It is worth noting, however, that the rate of increase is highest for full professors, so women's access to senior, tenured positions appears to be improving.

Finally, the percentage of employed engineers who are women also has increased steadily over the past 25 years. In 1993, women represented less than 10% of employed engineers; that percentage had risen above 10% by 2001, when the SWE Literature Review was first published. In the subsequent 20 years, women's share of engineering employment has continued to grow, rising to about 18% in 2019. It should be emphasized, however, that the rate of growth is very slow, and that women's share of engineering employment is substantially lower than women's share of engineering degrees.

## LOOKING BACK AT 20 YEARS OF SWE LITERATURE REVIEWS — WHAT WE'VE LEARNED

Our "meta-analysis" of two decades of literature reviews reveals that much research on women in engineering specifically, and STEM more broadly, has been focused on a finite set of questions. In what follows, we attempt to summarize what has been learned about those questions. We are encouraged to note that, over the years, researchers have learned a great deal about the reasons for women's underrepresentation in engineering and about the effectiveness (or ineffectiveness) of programs designed to promote change. Although we do not know everything we need to know, and important questions remain unresolved, one can point to a number of significant insights that are now well-established.

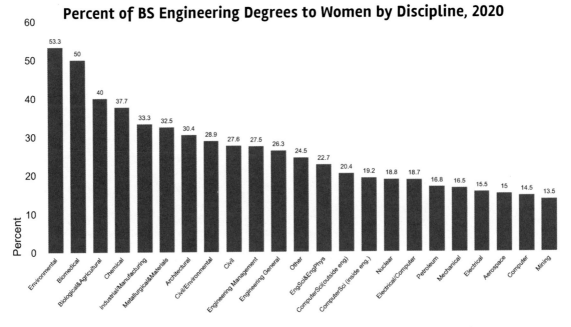

**Percent of BS Engineering Degrees to Women by Discipline, 2020**

(Source: ASEE (2021) Profiles of Engineering and Engineering Technology. Washington DC)

*It's Not Just About Math*

It was long thought that a primary obstacle to women's entry into engineering was math achievement. Until the last few decades, girls' average math achievement trailed boys' and advanced math classes in high schools (e.g., calculus) were disproportionately male. Since it remains the case that taking advanced math classes in high school is a strong predictor of majoring in engineering, the male/female math achievement "gap" was an obvious explanation for the small numbers of female engineering majors. This appeared so difficult an obstacle to overcome that researchers such as Sally Hacker raised questions about whether calculus was more of a gender barrier than an occupational requirement for practicing engineers.[ii]

The 2001 literature review still mentioned research showing that achievement gaps in math and science were a factor inhibiting women's entry into engineering. And, in 2005, the review discussed Lawrence Summers' infamous comments to the effect that women were less likely to have the aptitudes required to succeed in engineering; in his view, women's brains were "wired" differently,

meaning many lacked the innate ability to succeed in science and engineering.[iii] In the intervening years, however, research has shown that the gender gap has narrowed, at least in some respects. Although boys continue to outscore girls on standardized math tests of various kinds, advanced math classes such as calculus are no longer dominated by boys (if anything, the reverse may be true), and girls consistently earn higher grades than their male counterparts. Of course, the SWE Literature Review has summarized research emphasizing that there remains a gender gap at the "right tail" of the distribution — that is, boys are more likely than girls to score in the extremely high range of assessments of math ability and achievement.[iv] Some have argued that this remains a reason for the low numbers of women in engineering because they believe it is high achievers who are most likely to select engineering majors. However, other researchers have shown that boys with mediocre math scores are more likely to enter engineering than girls with very high math scores.[v] So, it may be that the composition of the "right tail" of the distribution is

*continued on page 15*

## Percent of BS Engineering Degrees to Women by Discipline, 2002

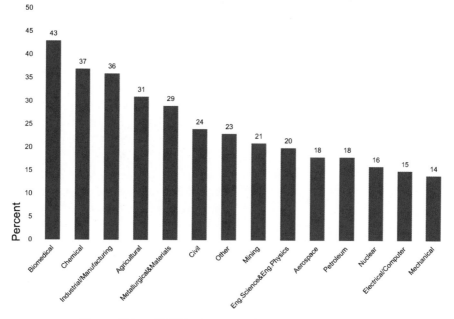

(Source: Gibbons (2003) Engineering on the Rise. ASEE. Washington DC)

# Two Recent Books Provide Insights from Navigating the Status Quo to Critical Analysis

Scientific research is an activity that has been largely dominated by men. Although some academic science disciplines have gradually become somewhat more gender integrated (in 2019, just over 40% of doctorate holders employed in academic biology, agriculture, and other life science departments were women, National Science Foundation 2021), most scientific disciplines remain heavily male dominated (in 2019 fewer than 25% of doctorate holders employed in academic physical science departments were women, ibid.). Despite a small number of notable exceptions, such as Marie Curie, Ph.D.; Barbara McClintock, Ph.D.; and Rosalind Franklin, Ph.D., few female scientists have achieved wide public recognition. As of 2020, only 23 women had been awarded a Nobel Prize in a science discipline, and more than half of those have been in physiology or medicine (Nobel Foundation 2021).

Two books published this year offer an opportunity to reflect on the changing role of women in academic science and scientific research. Walter Isaacson's (2021) biography of Jennifer Doudna, Ph.D., one of the researchers credited with developing the gene-editing technology CRISPR, provides a portrait of one of the few women to have been awarded a Nobel Prize in a scientific discipline. Chanda Prescod-Weinstein, Ph.D. (2021), the first woman of color to hold a tenure-track position in theoretical cosmology, offers a critical account of the role of gender, race, and sexual orientation in physics in *The Disordered Cosmos: A Journey into Dark Matter, Spacetime, and Dreams Deferred.* While Isaacson's portrait of Dr. Doudna shows how a woman was able to succeed in the "man's world" of science, Dr. Prescod-Weinstein argues that science (or at least physics) is profoundly shaped, indeed distorted by its domination by White males of European origin, making it a difficult place for women to thrive and limiting science's ability fully to understand the physical world.

## SUCCEEDING WITHIN THE STATUS QUO

Isaacson's biography of Dr. Doudna describes her developing an interest in biology, encouraged by nature walks with a family friend, while growing up in Hawaii. She did encounter some gender-based discouragement from a high school counselor, but she was able to overcome this and to succeed academically, benefiting along the way from working with female professors. She became interested in RNA (rather than DNA) while doing graduate work at Harvard; Isaacson describes her as determined to understand the molecule's shape, inspired in part by the pioneering structural biological work done by Rosalind Franklin. This eventually led to her interest in CRISPR. Scientists had noticed that bacterial DNA developed repeated sequences that matched those of the viruses that attacked them, allowing them to acquire an immunity to those attacks. Dr. Doudna and others suspected that this process worked through RNA interference (although this turned out not to be the case).

Dr. Doudna's subsequent research took place largely at Berkeley, where she and her team, in collaboration with French researcher Emmanuelle Charpentier, Ph.D., figured out how CRISPR–associated enzymes in bacteria cut DNA to replicate the sequences of the viruses that attack them. Dr. Doudna and her group eventually learned to simplify the process by which these enzymes operate, developing a method that did not occur naturally in bacteria. They eventually published a paper on their results in *Science* in 2012. As with many scientific breakthroughs, Drs. Doudna and Charpentier's work did not occur in isolation; other scientists were working simultaneously on the same matters, and Isaacson documents in some detail the disputes that arose over who discovered what, and when. In the end, although other researchers were acknowledged to have made important contributions, it was Drs. Doudna and Charpentier who received the Nobel Prize for research leading to the development of CRISPR's gene editing technology.

Isaacson's account of Dr. Doudna's work acknowledges the masculine characteristics of research science. He describes the aggressive competition among researchers to receive credit for scientific discoveries. And, he notes how journal editors respond favorably to aggressive, self-promoting language in researchers' submissions. He also describes Dr. Doudna's concerns about anti-female bias among the venture capitalists who fund scientific startups and argues that she and

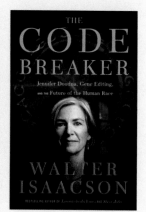

Jennifer Doudna, Ph.D., with a model of the CRISPR gene-editing tool.

her female collaborators' "self-awareness" and humility (not typical of alpha males) helped them to build a successful scientific team.

In the end, however, Isaacson's story is about Dr. Doudna's ability not to change this masculine world but to succeed within it. She was able to sidestep the venture capitalists by raising funds for her startup from family and friends. She held her own in the competition over who should receive credit for discoveries and earn patents. And she was not reluctant to promote her work using the kinds of language (e.g., describing discoveries as "unique," "unprecedented," and "novel") that aggressive male researchers often used. Dr. Doudna undoubtedly benefited from not being alone, from the fact that biology is a field in which there are significant numbers of female researchers from whom she could learn and with whom she could collaborate. But, Isaacson's biography makes clear that Dr. Doudna's success in no way changed the gendered character of research science. If one accepts the implications of his account, more women will earn Nobel Prizes in science if and when they learn to emulate the behaviors of successful male scientists.

## MAKING THE CASE FOR A TRANSFORMATION IN SCIENCE

Chanda Prescod-Weinstein, Ph.D.'s critical account of her experiences as a female physicist of color makes a very different case, arguing forcefully that science

(not women) must change and that science, as well as women, will benefit from that transformation. While her wide-ranging book describes her (and others') experiences of gender- and race-based discrimination and harassment in physics, her aim is to make a case for doing more than increasing the numbers of women and people of color in physics:

> "… it is not enough to repopulate history. Not only should we ask where the hidden figures are, but also what they were doing and what agendas they were serving. We must reimagine Physics through a Black feminist frame." (268)

Dr. Prescod-Weinstein (2021) describes the many ways in which the culture of physics is dominated by White men and a Western European tradition. She argues that women and people of color are rarely acknowledged within physics and are much less likely to be encouraged to ask "big questions." She notes that academic "housework" (all the non-research tasks, from cleaning to advising undergraduates) typically falls on people who aren't White men and that academic administrators worry about how efforts to increase diversity may compromise "excellence," implying thereby that only White men can be excellent. She also points to a telling irony in the ways in which complaints about discrimination are received:

*sidebar continued on page 14*

*sidebar continued from page 13*

Chanda Prescod–Weinstein, Ph.D.

"Black women are constantly asked to provide hard evidence for our evaluations of our most common-place experiences with discrimination, yet white men are taken seriously when they suggest that more affirming data isn't necessary in order to test their theories of quantum gravity." (170)

She obviously believes that it is important to increase diversity in physics; indeed, she complains that too many efforts to argue for diversity focus on the needs of the nation (staying competitive, filling shortages of personnel) rather than on the needs of women and people of color. But, for this to happen, science itself must change. Dr. Prescod-Weinstein notes how the very substance of physics is shaped by its White, male culture. For example, the theory known as quantum chromodynamics (which uses color as analogy for physical properties unrelated to color) is sometimes referred to in textbooks as "colored physics," a term unlikely to have been adopted if physics were more diverse.

Her contention is that diversifying physics also will involve and require reconsidering its relationship to society. Equating science as currently constructed with "progress" ignores the ways in which science can and does trample on the rights of native peoples (as in the construction of a telescope on sacred lands in Hawaii) and erases the contributions of non–White males to knowledge. Research will be driven not simply by the priorities of dominant groups (e.g., interest in

physics of melanin will not be rooted only in concern about protecting White people from skin cancer). Dr. Prescod-Weinstein feels that diversifying physics will both require and enable a questioning of science's relationship to social institutions such as colonialism and militarism. The result, she concludes, will be enhanced knowledge of the physical world:

"Only time, and a community that does not have extensive barriers to the participation of people from a broad cross section of humanity, will be able to tell how our understanding of physics will change when our understanding of who can be a physicist changes." (26)

### References

*National Science Foundation (2021).* Women, Minorities and Persons with Disabilities in Science and Engineering. *Table 9-28, Science, Engineering, and Health Doctorate Holders Employed in Universities and 4-year Colleges, by Broad Occupation, Sex, Race, Ethnicity, and Faculty Rank: 2019.*

*Nobel Foundation (2021). The Nobel Prize: Women Who Changed the World. https://bit.ly/3Ja31s9*

*Isaacson, W. (2021).* The Code Breaker: Jennifer Doudna, Gene Editing, and the Future of the Human Race. *New York: Simon and Schuster.*

*Prescod-Weinstein, C. (2021).* The Disordered Cosmos: A Journey into Dark Matter, Spacetime, and Dreams Deferred. *New York: Bold Type Books.*

continued from page 11

not the central issue. And, other research finds that girls who are high achievers in math are significantly less likely to choose an engineering major than boys with similar levels of math achievement.[vi] One possible reason is that high-achieving girls, in contrast to many high-achieving boys, are high achievers in *other* fields besides math, meaning that they have broader options in choosing a major and career.[vii] Overall, changes in the nature of the gender achievement gap in math have led to a decreased emphasis in the research literature on the role of math achievement in limiting the numbers of women in engineering.

There is, however, another way in which researchers continue to find a relationship between girls' math experiences and their interest in majoring in engineering. The SWE Literature Review has discussed a large body of research that had begun to develop as early as 2001 focused on whether girls are less confident in math than their male counterparts. With a high level of consistency, research on this question finds that, when compared with boys with similar levels of achievement in math, girls tend to evaluate themselves lower.[viii]

Whether there is a causal link between this lower self-evaluation and deciding not to major in engineering is somewhat less clear. It seems reasonable to suppose that it may affect girls' confidence in being successful in engineering and that it may contribute to their feeling that engineering is not for them (a theme we discuss below). However, research published in 2021 found that even girls who hold the counter-stereotypical view that girls are better at math than boys are *not* more likely to major in physical sciences and engineering, although they *are* more likely to major in biology.[ix]

In sum, while substantial research effort has been and continues to be expended on examining whether math and/or confidence in math affect girls' interest in majoring in engineering, the relationship among math achievement, math confidence, and interest in engineering appears to be, at best, complex. It is perhaps time to agree with a study by Isaacs, summarized in the very first SWE Literature Review, that argued that "recruiting efforts directed toward encouraging girls to study math and science are focused on the wrong problem." (4)[x]

## Not All Women Are the Same

Research on women in engineering has introduced the term *intersectionality* to capture the reality that talking about "women in engineering" as if all women shared the same experiences is a serious mistake. The SWE Literature Review has discussed a growing body of research that details the ways in which a woman's race or ethnicity can affect her experience in engineering, the ways in which sexual orientation can matter and, most recently, the different experiences of female engineers with disabilities. There has been far too much research to summarize it all adequately here. A few examples of the kinds of insights attention to intersectionality has yielded will have to suffice.

Research published in 2021 illustrates well the value of attending to the different experiences of female engineers of different races and ethnicities. Cross et al. (2021) describe the fact that female students of color face a "double bind" in which they are continually required to dispel negative stereotypes based on their group association (i.e., both their race/ethnicity and their gender) and to defend their presence within the engineering culture.[xi] True-Funk et al. (2021) conducted a set of interviews with a diverse group of engineering undergraduates, documenting their experience of microaggressions and finding a variety of intersectional effects — the consequences for African American women differed somewhat from those for African American men, differed again from the effects on Latina or Latino students, and so on.[xii] Interestingly, True-Funk et al.'s research, like a small-scale interview study (Ross, Huff, and Godwin 2021) of nine successful, *senior* engineers of color (all had been in the field for at least 10 years), found that African American women, despite the "double bind" they faced, were able to make their racial identity into a strength and to find ways to make it congruent with their identity as engineers.[xiii]

Earlier research described in the literature review emphasized the need to tailor recruitment efforts to the different experiences and situations of students of color. For example, efforts to increase the number of female students of color need to address those students' desire to help their communities and take advantage of the peer support groups students themselves form and on which they rely. Efforts to recruit them also need to recognize that they are likely to attend schools that don't support the students' language and culture (thus weakening their resilience) and are less likely to provide them with the math and science instruction they need to succeed in engineering. Recruitment efforts also need to recognize that many students of color begin their educations in two-year institutions and make an effort to build pipelines from those schools to four-year engineering programs.[xiv] Sexual orientation has been identified as another axis of intersectionality affecting women in engineering. Yang et al. (2021) report on a focus group study of nine LGBTQ+ engineering students at a large public university in the Southeast. Their respondents report feelings of isolation (even if there were other women in their classes), the need to respond continually to homophobic comments and behaviors, and how they deliberately sought out institutional roles (such as being a TA) that would enable them to help other

LGBTQ+ students find the resources they needed.[xv] Finally, an interesting study reviewed in 2017 noted the ways in which gender, sexual orientation, and race all intersected to produce a range of different experiences for female engineers. The 18 tech workers in the Bay Area all reported struggling to fit into the male "geek culture" that shaped their workplaces. However, their identities affected their ability to succeed. White women whose self-presentation was "gender fluid" and who identified as LGBTQ were better able than others to manage their status on male-dominated teams. Race mattered, however, as black LGBTQ women were not as successful.[xvi]

These are merely a few examples of the many interesting insights produced by a focus on intersectionality. What this research illustrates is that a "one-size-fits-all" approach to promoting gender equity in engineering is unlikely to be successful. Happily, a retrospective look at the SWE Literature Review demonstrates that researchers and advo-

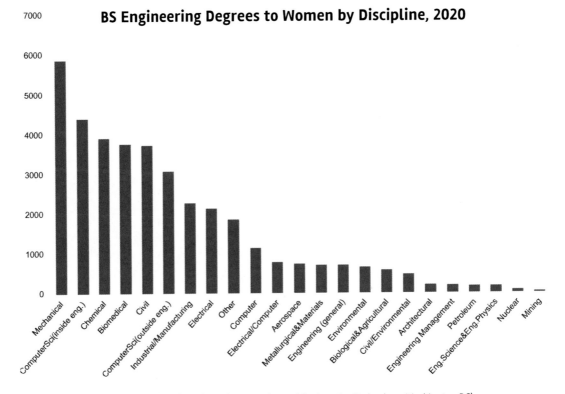

**BS Engineering Degrees to Women by Discipline, 2020**

(Source: ASEE (2021) Profiles of Engineering and Engineering Technology. Washington DC)

cates for gender equity in engineering have become increasingly aware of the need to understand and take into account the differences among the many kinds of women in engineering.

### Recruitment Needs to be Combined with Retention

The "leaky pipeline" metaphor has been criticized for oversimplifying the process by which women make their way into and progress through engineering careers. However, researchers acknowledge that it is important to examine not just which methods of recruitment promise to increase the numbers of women in engineering, but also what needs to be done to ensure that they remain. If large numbers of women leave the profession at some point during their life course, even the most vigorous recruitment efforts are likely to have little effect on engineering's gender balance.

One could argue that there is a sense in which girls leave the profession before they even enter it! Research reviewed in 2020 found that both male and female students' interest in STEM declined during the high school years, but that girls' interest in science and engineering tends to decline much faster.[xvii] Since the numbers of girls with engineering intentions are small to begin with, this pattern of decline is an obvious reason for the underrepresentation of women in college engineering programs.

There has been much discussion of the retention of women in college programs. Many studies describe the fact that some female students leave engineering majors, but many of these studies, including some of the most carefully done[xviii], don't include male students in their analysis. Since male students leave engineering majors too, it would be necessary to show that women leave at higher rates than men to argue that the gender gap is the result of female attrition.

Whether women leave college engineering programs at higher rates than men has been much continued on page 20

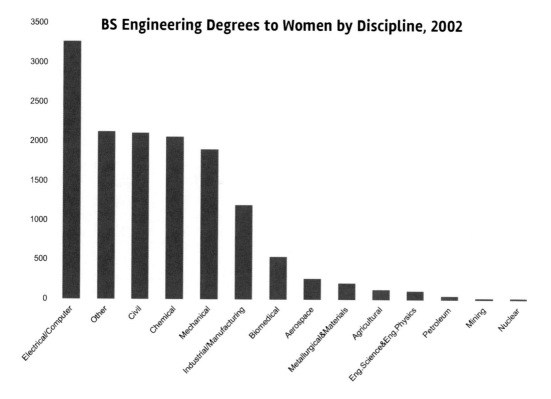

## BS Engineering Degrees to Women by Discipline, 2002

(Source: Gibbons (2003) Engineering on the Rise. ASEE. Washington DC)

# Sexism in the Gaming Industry: Are Things Beginning to Change?

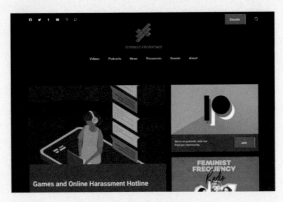

Games and Online Harassment Hotline

The tech industry has been the focus of critical attention for a number of years as a result of revelations that it is the site of widespread gender discrimination, sexual harassment, and sexual misbehavior of various sorts. *SWE Magazine* has reviewed a number of the most significant controversies in its annual State of Women in Engineering issue. A component of the tech sector that has received less attention here, but also has a history of controversies over sexual harassment and gender discrimination, is the gaming industry.

Over the past decade, news media reports have characterized gaming as a male-dominated industry in which women are in the minority and regularly experience harassment and mistreatment. The most recent case to receive public attention concerns Activision Blizzard. In 2021, the state of California filed suit against the company, the maker of World of Warcraft and other highly successful games, accusing it of repeated cases of sexual harassment and discrimination against its female employees. An investigation found a "frat boy" environment at the company in which men joked about rape, male superiors harassed female employees, and drunken male employees engaged in "cube crawls" harassing female workers.

Critics cite evidence of misbehavior dating back to 2013, including the hosting of women by a senior manager in a hotel room named the "Cosby suite" and other Cosby-related "jokes" by employees. The company's CEO is alleged to have known about the problems for years, to have done nothing about it, and to have participated himself in the sexual harassment and discrimination. Thirteen-hundred employees of the company have petitioned, calling for the CEO's resignation (Reymann-Schneider 2021; Kassorla 2021).

This is not an isolated case that came out of nowhere. Controversies over sexism in the industry have a long history, including accusations that female gamers are marginalized and harassed and other incidents in which employers have been accused of mistreating female employees. The problem exploded onto the public stage in 2014 as a result of the so-called Gamergate incident, in which videogame developer Zoë Quinn became the subject of a disparaging blog, eventually leading to death threats, doxing, and hate speech directed at her and other women by male members of the gaming community. One woman had to leave home when her personal information was made public, and she received death threats.

Although some continue to claim that the attacks on Quinn and others were about ethics in the industry, all of the people attacked were women, in an industry in which women are a small minority of employees (Kassorla 2021; MacDonald 2020). Observers claim that Gamergate cemented an aggressive masculine culture in the industry; it also spurred the work of industry critic Anita Sarkeesian (also a target of Gamergate), who earlier had established Feminist Frequency, a platform that disseminates educational materials and provides outlets for those involved in the industry to give voice to complaints about gender discrimination and harassment (Zenerations 2021).

In the aftermath of Gamergate, a number of incidents kept sexism in gaming in the spotlight. In 2019, an investigation by the video game website Kotaku led to a gender discrimination lawsuit against game company Riot Games. This resulted in a payment of $10 million to the company's female employees, whose CEO was also investigated for sexual harassment, although he was eventually acquitted. In 2020, French developer Ubisoft faced accusations of harassment and discrimination, especially in its Toronto and Montreal offices. A number of senior employees wound up resigning and the company's CEO publicly pledged to reform the company's culture (Garcia 2021; MacDonald 2020).

### HAVE WE REACHED A TIPPING POINT?
Game players (gamers) have also been accused of sexual misbehavior. An article in *The New York Times* in 2020 drew attention to a rash of accusations by women against male streamers in the online gaming world.

First in 2019, then again in 2020, women made public allegations of harassment, gender-based discrimination, and assault on various online platforms. The 2020 outburst began in response to a tweet by a female gamer accusing a "top player" of the online game Destiny of being a "scum lord." Others posted similar accounts in response, and the accused gamer eventually apologized. More streamers began opening up about their experiences, and Jessica Richey compiled these stories into a Twitter thread. Many of the 2020 accusations focused on the streaming platform Twitch, which acknowledged the accusations and said it was looking into the matter. Some streamers have called for a boycott of Twitch (Lorenz and Browning 2020).

Many have asked why sexist behavior is so widespread in the gaming industry. Researchers have noted that gaming has long been stereotyped as a male activity. At least since an economic downturn in the industry in the 1980s, game companies have identified men as their primary customers and targeted them in designing popular games. Researcher Kenzie Gordon, quoted in *The New York Times*, says that men have "created the identity of the gamer as this exclusive property" (Lorenz and Browning 2020). Although there is evidence that women, too, are involved in gaming and that the stereotype of the male "geek" gamer is not particularly accurate, female game players are often dismissed by male gamers as not serious and less skilled. Even e-sport participants are affected by the industry's male orientation, as only one of the 500 top-earning professionals is a woman, and critics accuse female tournaments of offering much lower prize money than male events (Paaßen, Morgenroth, and Stratemeyer 2017; Garcia 2021).

Male domination of the industry, and its focus on its male customers, has led to the production of video games with few female characters and the hypersexualization of the few there are, although there is some evidence that this has begun to change (Lynch et al. 2016). It also has been linked to the development of a male workplace culture that is conducive to sexual abuse. A recent article in *The Guardian* quoted Emily Greer, CEO of Double Loop Games, to that effect:

> "Many of the workplace risk factors cited by the US Equal Employment Opportunity Commission are commonplace in the games industry: overwhelming male workforce; lots of young workers; workplaces where some 'superstar' employees are perceived to be particularly valuable; workplaces with significant power disparities; and workplaces which endorse alcohol consumption" (MacDonald 2020).

The reaction to the most recent accusations of sexism in the industry has led some to be optimistic, to speculate that a tipping point may have been reached, and that real change is possible. They are encouraged to see that, instead of the usual backlash, recent incidents have elicited sympathetic responses and have led to resignations and pledges by company CEOs to reform the culture. In some cases, companies have brought in expensive consultants and hired diversity officers as part of their efforts to reform. Others are less certain, arguing that change is not likely to occur in a top-down manner. They feel it needs to come from those affected, and that it must involve radical change, not just reform (MacDonald 2020). Perhaps these skeptics would be encouraged by a recent interview with the female game director of German game design company Wooga, who points to the successful diversification of its workforce and who emphasizes what she characterizes as growing calls *within* the industry for change (Reymann-Schneider 2021).

### References

Garcia, J. (2021). *The Video Game Industry Faces Another Reckoning over Sexism.* El Pais, Aug. 27.

Kassorla, M. (2021). *Sexism Within the Video Game Industry.* The Cornell Daily Sun, Aug. 30.

Lorenz, T. and Browning, K. (2020). *Dozens of Women in Gaming Speak out About Sexism and Harassment.* The New York Times, June 23.

Lynch, T. et al. (2016). *Sexy, Strong and Secondary: A Content Analysis of Female Characters in Video Games Across 31 Years.* Journal of Communication 66(4): 564–584.

MacDonald, K. (2020). *Is the Video Games Industry Finally Reckoning with Sexism?* The Guardian, July 22.

Paaßen, B., Morgenroth, T., and Stratemeyer, M. (2017). *What Is a True Gamer? The Male Gamer Stereotype and the Marginalization of Women in Video Game Culture.* Sex Roles 76: 421–435.

Reymann-Schneider, K. (2021). *Sexism and the Video Games Industry.* DW, Nov. 19.

Zenerations (2021). *Sexism in Gaming Communities.* Zenerations, July 21.

*continued from page 17*

disputed. Lisa Frehill, who led the SWE Literature Review project for most of its first decade, stated clearly in a 2010 publication that they did *not*[xix] Subsequent editions of the literature review have discussed a number of research studies of this question, but there continues to be no clear consensus as to how to answer it. In 2016, the review cited a meta-analysis of the research on attrition by Cheryan et al. that asserted strongly that recruitment, not retention, was the reason for the gender gap in engineering.[xx] Much of the subsequent research reviewed by SWE has been consistent with that conclusion, but occasional studies appear that continue to find evidence of a gender gap in retention. For example, research on major-switching published in 2021 found that women switched majors more frequently than men and were more likely to switch out of STEM majors.[xxi] A comprehensive national study of this issue may be needed to resolve the debate.

There is a higher level of consensus that women leave engineering *after* graduating at higher rates than men, especially since the percentage of engineering degrees earned by women is substantially higher, consistently, than the percentage of employed engineers who are women. There is somewhat less certainty as to *why* this attrition occurs, in part because of the limited amount of research being conducted on the experiences of working engineers. However, a number of possible reasons have been suggested.

Among the leading explanations of women's leaving engineering careers at higher rates than men involves work/family conflict. At least since the pioneering publication in 2004 of Anne Preston, *Leaving Science*,[xxii] researchers have emphasized how women find the time demands of engineering and scientific careers difficult to reconcile with their domestic responsibilities. Major studies by, among others, Fouad and Singh and Cech and Blair-Loy have documented further the effect of work/family conflict on women's persistence in engineering.[xxiii] *Failing Families, Failing Science*, a book on the issue published in 2016, did make the case that growing numbers of men also struggled with the time commitments required by careers in academic STEM, but it still acknowledged that women were more affected by work/family conflict than men.[xxiv]

Other research questions the centrality of work/family conflict to women's departure from engineering careers. An important example is

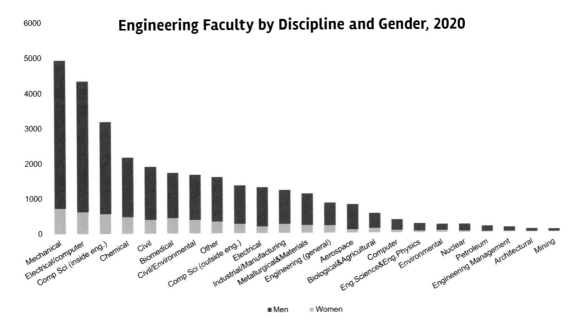

**Engineering Faculty by Discipline and Gender, 2020**

■ Men  ■ Women

(Source: ASEE (2021) Profiles of Engineering and Engineering Technology. Washington DC)

SWE's own study of why women leave engineering, the results of which were published in an issue of *SWE Magazine* in 2016.[xxv] This study found that work/family balance was not the primary reason for women's leaving. Instead, women left because they found themselves working in environments that tolerated persistent obstacles to their organizational and career goals. Fouad and Singh's research, while emphasizing work/family conflict, also noted that female engineers often left because their career goals were not being met.[xxvi]

An interesting study published in 2021 points to a possible reason why work/family conflict may *not* play as central a role as might be thought in causing midcareer women to leave engineering. Thébaud and Taylor (2021) conducted interviews with 57 postdocs and doctoral students in science and engineering, 2/3 of whom were women. Their respondents described a "specter of motherhood" in which motherhood was constructed in opposition to professional legitimacy, as something to fear. Female students and faculty (but not men) felt compelled to conceal motherhood and to choose between motherhood and career.[xxvii] This analysis suggests that some women may be leaving engineering *before* they embark on careers or that they find

ways either to avoid motherhood or to subordinate it to the careers to which they have committed.

Finally, many have mentioned women's experience of the masculine culture of engineering as a reason for their departure. The SWE Literature Review has discussed numerous publications describing that culture and some women's unwillingness to adapt to it (more on the masculine culture of engineering below). While much of that literature takes the form of anecdotal accounts of personal experiences, two well-conceived studies of the early-career experiences of female engineers show how male culture can push women away. Seron et al. (2016)[xxviii] studied a group of engineering students at four New England universities, finding that their experiences in internships and team projects already involved gender stereotyping that affected their enthusiasm for engineering careers. The 2016 literature review quoted that study as follows:

> "The findings reported here suggest that subtle and cumulative encounters with the values and norms of professional culture compromise women's affiliation with the profession and raise the prospect of departure." (pp. 30–31)

continued on page 24

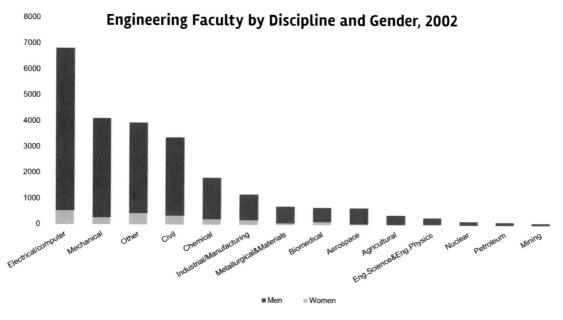

**Engineering Faculty by Discipline and Gender, 2002**

■ Men   ■ Women

(Source: Gibbons (2003) Engineering on the Rise. ASEE. Washington DC)

# Comparative and International Perspectives on Women in Engineering

Some of the research discussed in SWE's annual literature review concerns countries other than the United States. Of course, there is far more research on engineering outside the U.S. — SWE'S review discusses only research published in English, while most of the research on specific countries is published in the language of the country being studied. Still, the volume of international research SWE reviews is substantial, so it is worth giving some thought to its significance.

A few of the studies SWE has reviewed are truly comparative in nature, either comparing the situation of female engineers in a small number of countries, or, in some cases, developing a classification system into which a wide range of countries' experiences can be sorted. Studies such as these are made possible by the existence of large-scale data sets comparing information on a range of countries. Organizations such as the International Labour Organization (ILO) and the Organisation for Economic Co-operation and Development (OECD) are particularly important sources of this kind of comparative data. The latter's Programme for International Student Assessment (PISA) study, which measures 15-year-olds' ability to use their reading, mathematics, and science knowledge and skills to meet real-life challenges, has been a particularly important source for researchers in examining national differences in young people's aptitude in and orientation toward STEM disciplines.

Among truly comparative studies, one can mention the research, discussed in this year's literature review, exploring the relationship between the status of women in general in particular countries and the likelihood that women in those countries will pursue engineering majors and careers. Other examples include an article by Singh and Peers (2019) that classifies countries into four categories, then tries to use this system to note differences in women's participation in engineering. In 2021, Hägglund and Leuze analyzed the occupational expectations of 15-year-olds in 35 OECD countries. Using OECD data as well as data from the PISA data base (see above), they find that the gender gap in STEM career expectations is higher in countries where the post-industrial, service labor market is more highly developed, primarily because boys' STEM expectations in such countries were higher. Moe, Hausmann, and Hirnstein (2021) report on a comparative study of STEM students in three countries (Norway, the U.K., and Italy), finding that the likelihood that men and women will endorse gender stereotypes about various abilities is affected by the country's overall gender gap.

Comparative studies such as these can shed light on the differences between female engineers' experiences in various countries and help researchers and policymakers identify what is unique (and what is not) about the U.S. case. There are also many studies of individual countries, usually based on data collected by the researchers themselves or on publicly available data for the country in question. These studies are not written with an explicit comparative intent; indeed, in many cases, as with many studies using U.S. data, researchers discuss data specific to one country as if it applied to engineering everywhere. For U.S. readers, the principal value of these studies is to educate them about women's situation in engineering in other countries and to use this knowledge to put the U.S. situation in context.

Recently published research illustrates well what can be learned from national studies of this type. Beckmann's (2021) study of German adolescents reveals that the gender gap in STEM aspirations can be affected by classroom context. She finds that the gender gap in students' occupational expectations is larger in classrooms characterized by high mathematical expectations and aspirations toward STEM. In these classrooms, female students less frequently expect to work in STEM careers; male students *more* frequently. Beckmann does not offer suggestions as to what to do about this, nor does she suggest that her results are specific to the German context, but her results point to an issue that U.S. researchers may wish to consider.

Jasko et al.'s (2020) study of women in Polish engineering finds that they face a variety of challenges, including a salary gap, greater difficulty finding employment, and a greater likelihood of being employed in jobs inconsistent with their qualifications. As pointed out in the 2020 literature review, this is surprising in a country where women's share of science and engineering employment is much higher than in the U.S. (close to 48%) and indicates that simply increasing the numbers of women in U.S. engineering will not, by itself, guarantee gender equity. Rincon et al.'s (2019) report on SWE's study of women engineers in India highlights similarities and differences to the U.S. case, noting that Indian

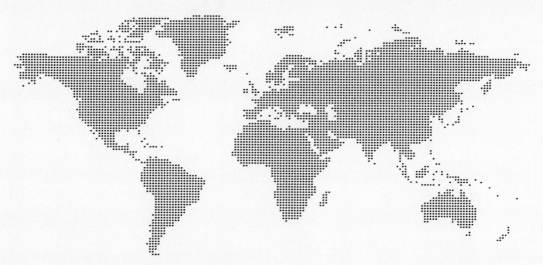

women engineers face many of the same challenges, but also encounter ones unique to India ("stop-go bias" and legislation intended to "protect" women from late night employment).

Having a comparative focus and an understanding of national differences is significant also because of the importance of international cooperation in achieving gender equity in engineering and science, not just in the U.S., but globally. There has been ongoing interest among engineering educators and others in learning from one another and collaborating on the work of increasing women's access to engineering and engineering equity more broadly. The 2007 literature review included a sidebar (Hill and Frehill 2007) describing the various forms international cooperation to encourage equity in engineering can take: from the establishment of Engineers Without Borders chapters, to the Fulbright program, to conferences at which scholars can share information about the experiences of their country, etc. Work such as this that reaches across national borders continues, including the work of SWE itself, which has conducted research internationally and holds events including roundtables and regional conferences in various countries. International collaboration by scientists and engineers can also be an important element in professional development. Researchers have found that women, particularly in the United States, are less likely than their male counterparts to be successful in developing those international collaborations, so having a greater understanding of how engineering and science are organized in various countries, and women's place within that, can be an important tool in promoting women's careers in engineering and science (Zippel 2017; Fox et al. 2017).

## References

Beckmann, J. (2021). Gendered Career Expectations in Context: the Relevance of Normative and Comparative Reference Groups. British Journal of Sociology of Education 42(7): 968–88.

Fox, M.F., M.L. Realff, D.R. Rueda, and J. Morn (2017). International Research Collaboration Among Women Engineers: Frequency and Perceived Barriers, by Regions. The Journal of Technology Transfer 42(6): 1292–1306.

Hägglund, A.E. and K. Leuze (2021). Gender Differences in STEM Expectations Across Countries: How Perceived Labor Market Structures Shape Adolescents' Preferences. Journal of Youth Studies 24(5): 634–54.

Hill, S. and L. Frehill (2007). International Perspectives on Engineering Education. A Compendium of the SWE Annual Literature Reviews on Women in Engineering: 116.

Jasko, K., J. Pyrkosz-Pacyna, G. Czarnek, K. Dukała, and M. Szastok (2020). The STEM Graduate: Immediately After Graduation, Men and Women Already Differ in Job Outcomes, Attributions for Success, and Desired Job Characteristics. Journal of Social Issues 76(3): 512–542.

Moè, A., M. Hausmann, and M. Hirnstein (2021). Gender Stereotypes and Incremental Beliefs in STEM and Non-STEM students in Three Countries: Relationships with Performance in Cognitive Tasks. Psychological Research 85(2): 554–67.

Rincon, R., R.M. Korn, and J.C. Williams (2019). Examining Gender Bias in Engineering in India. ASEE Annual Conference and Exposition, Tampa, Fla.

Singh, S. and S.M.C. Peers (2019). Where Are the Women in the Engineering Labour Market? A Cross-Sectional Study. International Journal of Gender, Science and Technology 11(1).

Zippel, K. (2017). Women in Global Science: Advancing Academic Careers Through International Collaboration. Stanford, Calif.: Stanford University Press.

continued from page 21

In 2018, the literature review discussed a fascinating study by Wynn and Correll involving observation of recruiting sessions by technology companies at prominent West coast universities.[xxix] These recruiting sessions were consciously planned to recruit female candidates, but the study found that the primary presenters were generally male and that the presentations involved frequent (positive) references to the workplaces' fraternity-like cultures and to aspects of pop culture more likely to be of interest to men. Without intending to, the sessions may have been pushing women *away* from careers in technology.

In sum, while many questions remain about the timing of and reasons for women's departure from science and engineering, researchers have demonstrated clearly that retention, not just recruitment, is an important cause of the under-representation of women.

### Well-Funded, Sustained Programming Works — the Case of NSF-ADVANCE

The 2002 SWE Literature Review announced the initiation of NSF-ADVANCE, a federal program designed to support efforts to increase the numbers of female faculty in science and engineering, and noted that the first nine grants had been made. A new cohort of 10 projects was announced in the 2004 review. Since then, the literature review has regularly featured descriptions and assessments of individual NSF-ADVANCE projects as well as a number of overviews and analyses of the program as a whole.

These analyses of NSF-ADVANCE projects have, by and large, been positive, and it is clear that the work done in the various individual projects has gradually accumulated into real collective knowledge about the experiences of female faculty in STEM departments and about what works (and what does not) in supporting efforts to improve the recruitment and retention of women in academic STEM. Early assessments of NSF-ADVANCE projects emphasized the now familiar idea that departmental climate is important to both male and female faculty and that the impact of a toxic climate was greater on women.[xxx] Research summarized in 2010 identified a number of problems associated with traditional searches and techniques to overcome them, many of which have become standard practices in universities across the country.[xxxi] In 2012, the review discussed a book by Bilimoria and Liang that assessed the results of the first two ADVANCE cohort projects; that assessment was largely positive and emphasized that the

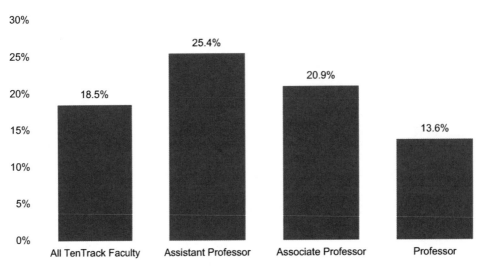

## Women as Percent of Tenured/Tenure–track Faculty by Rank, 2020

All TenTrack Faculty: 18.5%
Assistant Professor: 25.4%
Associate Professor: 20.9%
Professor: 13.6%

(Source: ASEE (2021) Profiles of Engineering and Engineering Technology. Washington DC)

programs' success was rooted in their having senior administrative support and involvement, the presence of an institutional champion, collaborative leadership, widespread and synergistic participation across campus, and the existence of visible actions and outcomes. Bilimoria and Liang also noted that a network of peer institutions had developed through ADVANCE and that the funding provided by NSF gave the programs legitimacy.[xxxii] Many more assessments of individual projects echo the conclusion that ADVANCE projects have had a significant impact on the institutions where they were implemented. An article published in 2021 even argued that a concept as important and ubiquitous as "implicit bias" took root in the broader corporate world largely because of pathbreaking work in projects supported by NSF-ADVANCE.[xxxiii]

The SWE Literature Review has discussed some criticisms of NSF ADVANCE. An assessment by Morimoto and Zajicek reviewed in 2014 noted that ADVANCE programs can be too focused on individuals (through mentoring programs and the like) and that they often rely on women to become the changemakers.[xxxiv] Zippel and Ferree, while praising ADVANCE in many respects, note that it has been limited in some ways by its need to balance the conflicting priorities of gender equity, organizational priorities, and the norms of scientific publication.[xxxv] Still, despite these criticisms, a re-reading of the research on NSF-ADVANCE discussed in the SWE Literature Review indicates that it has been a successful program that has had a significant impact on diversity in academic science and engineering. While it would be wrong to conclude that the growing share of academic positions in STEM held by women is entirely the result of NSF-ADVANCE programs, it also is obvious that the knowledge generated by ADVANCE projects has had effects well beyond the institutions at which they were implemented and has helped to spur the gradually increasing diversity of the STEM professoriate. NSF ADVANCE demonstrates that change can be promoted by well-funded national programs that combine good research with strong, internal support for sustained institutional transformation.

## AN ONGOING DEBATE

Thus, 20 years of research on women in engineering has resulted in real knowledge and in the exploration of new research questions — our understanding of the situation of women in engineering has definitely advanced. Yet, there is

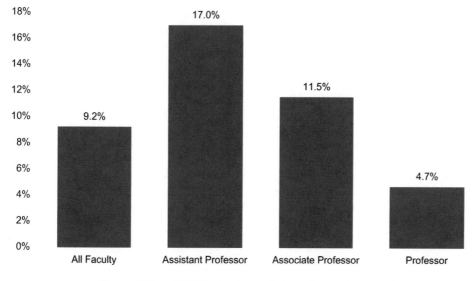

## Women as Percent of Tenured/Tenure-track Faculty by Rank, 2002

(Source: Gibbons (2003) Engineering on the Rise. ASEE. Washington DC)

a sense in which the arguments reviewed in 2021 would seem familiar to someone living in 2001. Specifically, researchers continue to be divided on the question of whether efforts to increase the numbers of women in engineering should focus on better preparing women for engineering as it currently exists, or whether gender equity in the field requires that engineering itself change in some way. In 2001, the year in which the first SWE Literature Review was published, Pamela Mack wrote an article titled "What Difference Has Feminism Made to Engineering in the Twentieth Century?"[xxxvi] She noted the question identified above, and concluded that, for the most part, researchers and program designers were not focused on changing engineering itself:

> "Rather than tackle subtle prejudice head on, studies of how to encourage more women to study engineering came to emphasize networking, mentoring and career development programs." (p. 159)

While the most popular strategies for encouraging women to study engineering have changed somewhat in the past 20 years, Mack's 2001 assessment could easily be applied to the situation in 2021. As our "meta-analysis" reveals, the relatively slow progress toward gender equity in engineering continues to fuel calls for a focus on structural changes, not just supporting individuals.

### Why Aren't Girls More Interested in Engineering and What Can Be Done About It?

A large portion of the research reviewed in SWE's Literature Review each year focuses on girls and women themselves: What do they think and what do they want? The hope seems to be that, if we can understand the psychological and motivational barriers to girls' involvement in engineering, we may be able to strengthen them in areas where they may be weak as potential engineers and to persuade them that they can fulfill themselves in the field. Research has shown that girls' and boys' interests develop early in life, so the focus has been on girls' development and experiences prior to their entering university.

Young girls' lack of knowledge about and experience with engineering is one recurring theme in research on their interest in the field. Researchers find that girls know relatively little about engineers and engineering, and that what they "know" is sometimes incorrect. For example, Salas-Morera et al. (2021) report on research in which they asked a sample of high school students whether engineers perform various tasks — some of the students were wrong, with more girls than boys being misinformed.[xxxvii] Girls have little contact with the field and are unlikely to have encountered female engineers whom they can emulate or from whom they can learn. Toys designed for girls typically do not encourage the development of the kinds of skills associated with engineering (building, tinkering, electronics, etc.) and parents are less likely to see their daughters as possessing the skills and inclinations that lead toward engineering, so they are less likely to encourage girls than boys in that direction.[xxxviii] All of this would seem to suggest that exposing girls early to engineering might help. But, as Cheryan et al. have noted, some fields where girls also do not have early exposure are actually female-dominated, so early experience alone may not be the solution.[xxxix]

Still, engineering continues to be perceived by both children and their parents as "masculine," as a field dominated by men and to which men are better suited than women. When Americans, both male and female, are asked to describe an engineer, they are much more likely to describe a man, a fact which affects young girls as well. One study reviewed in 2018 found that even incoming female undergraduate engineering *majors* viewed the "typical" engineer as stereotypically masculine.[xl] While this did not prevent these women from choosing to major in engineering, it seems likely that this stereotype is a factor steering other women away from the field. And, researchers have found that boys are particularly tenacious in defending gender norms, policing gender "deviants" strictly and aggressively claiming particular kinds of tasks as belonging to boys.[xli]

Researchers find that the perception that engineering is "male" affects girls' sense of belonging in the field, meaning they are less likely to aspire to a career in engineering or to persist in pursuing engineering studies should they begin. For example, Veldman's 2021 study of a sample of Belgian high school students in STEM-focused university tracks found that girls' concerns about "belonging" were significantly higher in fields (such as engineering) that are heavily male-dominated.[xlii]

Many Americans also link engineering and masculinity through the perception that being successful in the field involves "brilliance" and that brilliance is a quality that boys are more likely to have than girls. The SWE Literature Review has discussed numerous studies documenting the male-brilliance-engineering association, including one that found it developing very early — among children as young as 6![xliii] The 2020 review included a sidebar on Lisa Piccirillo, a mathematician who solved what had been seen as an insoluble math problem and has subsequently spoken out against the perception that innate brilliance is a requirement for success in math-intensive fields.

Researchers also have argued that girls have different interests and career goals than boys and that engineering typically does not present itself as a good field in which to pursue those interests and goals, even though it could easily make that case. In 2015, the literature review reported on Su and Rounds' meta-analysis of gender differences in interest as an explanation of the underrepresentation of women in STEM; it found that most studies confirmed that women were more interested in people-oriented than object-oriented fields, so disciplines such as engineering were seen as less attractive.[xliv]

Even studies of engineering *majors* seem to confirm the argument that young women are attracted by different aspects of a field than men. Erin Cech's study of undergraduate engineering students at four universities in the Northeast found that women's self-concepts led them to value social consciousness more and to be less likely to value technological leadership.[xlv] Similarly, Patrick, Riegle-Crumb, and Borrego[xlvi] report this year on a study of a sample of engineering students at a large public university in the United States, finding that men identified with engineering more strongly than women and that men identified with different aspects of engineering than women did. However, not all research confirms that differences in interest explain the failure of engineering to attract more female students. In 2019, the review discussed several research studies examining whether male and female students' interests differed.[xlvii] A number found that they did — women were found to be more people-oriented, interested in solving social problems, and altruistic. But another study found that it was quite common for both male and female STEM students to major in disciplines that did not align with their stated interests.[xlviii]

The overall effect of this type of research is to underline the fact that girls need to be *recruited* to engineering, while boys do not. Simply improving girls' math and science skills is not enough. Girls (and their parents and peers) need to be persuaded that engineering is for girls as well and that they can pursue their interests and career goals in the field. So, what do researchers and policymakers think might work?

One common suggestion is that having more female role models would help. The hope is that if girls have contact with more female engineers and encounter more women as they proceed through engineering programs, they will be more likely to aspire to engineering careers and persist in engineering programs and less likely to avoid the field because it seems male-dominated. Over the years, the SWE Literature Review has discussed numerous accounts of programs designed to bring young women into contact with female engineering role models, but the results of these programs vary, so the jury is still out on how effective they can be in increasing girls' interest in engineering.

Mentoring also is often mentioned as a strategy for increasing the numbers of women in engineering — here the emphasis is on *retaining* interested female students rather than recruiting the reluctant. Early issues of the literature review contained frequent reference to this strategy, including extended discussions in both the 2006 and 2008 reviews[xlix]. And, studies of the efficacy of mentoring and calls for expanded and improved mentoring for women at all stages of engineering careers continue to appear. There seems to be a consensus that effective mentoring helps women who enter engineering to persist and succeed, although the 2009 review summarized an article in *Research in Higher Education* that identified expanded mentoring as one of the "least successful" programs for undergraduate women in engineering.[l] However, researchers continue to examine questions such as whether female or male mentors are preferable, whether formal or informal mentors are more effective, whether women seek the same kind of mentoring as men, and how to avoid the reality that mentoring experiences can also be negative.

Some efforts to combat the perception of science and engineering as male focus on trying to strengthen girls' science or engineering identity. It seems logical to argue that, since, on average, girls identify less with science and engineering than boys, strengthening that identity would increase the likelihood that girls would enter and persist in engineering and science programs. Research has raised questions about whether a successful effort to do this will actually help. A study reviewed in 2020 found that science identity was more strongly associated with science aspirations for boys than for girls.[li] The fact that girls with strong science identities were less likely than comparable boys to aspire to science careers challenges the view that targeting girls' identities *alone* will increase their desire to pursue careers in science or engineering.

Perhaps the way to counter the cultural associa-

tion of engineering with masculinity is to present engineering differently. As we have seen, many researchers focus on the idea that girls have different interests and aspirations than boys and that engineering needs to do a better job of appealing to them. Some have suggested that a good way to do this would be to expand programs that already appeal to more women, such as environmental or biomedical engineering. However, research indicates that doing so tends to have the effect of drawing women away from other subdisciplines rather than increasing the numbers of women overall; it may even have the effect of hardening gender stereotypes within engineering, as fields such as mechanical or electrical engineering become even more male-dominated.[lii]

Researchers also have found varying answers to the question of whether engineering enables women (and men) to satisfy their "agentic" or communal goals. Some find support for the idea that engineering *can* be presented as a career in which such goals can be met, but others respond that it doesn't always do so. In either case, it is important

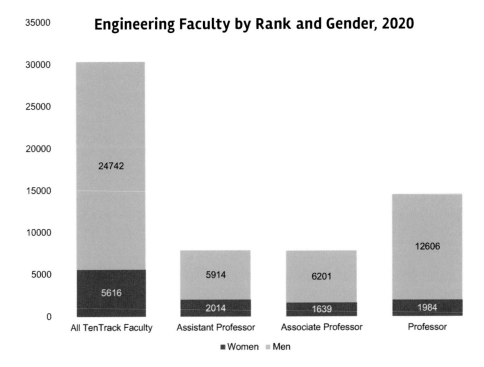

**Engineering Faculty by Rank and Gender, 2020**

(Source: ASEE (2021) Profiles of Engineering and Engineering Technology. Washington DC)

to take note of a study discussed in the 2018 review, which criticized what some see as cosmetic innovations in engineering's self-presentation; women are not likely to be persuaded to enter or to remain in the field if promises of a different approach are not sustained throughout engineering programs and careers.[liii]

Finally, researchers have shown that there is a need to be cautious in assuming that there is a simple relationship between individuals' stated goals and interests at a point in time and their career choices. As we saw above, there is evidence that many people in STEM fields have stated interests different from those associated with the careers they chose. And, other research has found that people adapt to the goals and values of the careers they select — women, in particular, may find that emphasizing communal goals is at odds with the prevailing male culture of engineering, so downplaying those goals and assimilating to traditional engineering culture may be viewed as a prudent career choice.[liv]

### Fix the System, Not the Women — What's Pushing Women Away?

Pamela Mack's 2001 analysis cited earlier argued that efforts to recruit girls and young women to engineering tended to focus on changing women — by educating them about the field, by persuading them that it offers them opportunities to fulfill their goals, and by strengthening their science and engineering identities. Over the succeeding 20 years, as the above review indicates, that emphasis has continued to inform much of the research on gender inequity and programmatic efforts to increase the numbers of women in the field. But, Mack's analysis noted that there is another way to approach the problem — perhaps it is engineering itself, and not just the women it seeks to attract, that needs to change if it is to become a field to which similar numbers of men and women are drawn. That approach has also continued to inform the work of some researchers and program designers, as the limits of focusing exclusively on women became apparent.

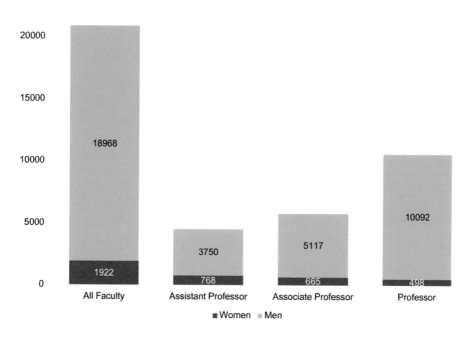

(Source: Gibbons (2003) Engineering on the Rise. ASEE. Washington DC)

Educated women in the United States have choices about which careers to enter; the evidence is that many of them are choosing more gender-integrated occupations. Pearlman's (2019) research showed that women are gravitating toward expanding opportunities in areas such as management, rather than trying to enter occupations that have been historically male-dominated, such as engineering.[lv] While she leaves open the question of whether women have a negative view of fields such as engineering, the reality that they can choose easy-to-enter, growing areas of employment, rather than overcome historical barriers to entry in engineering, tips the balance away from the latter. And, researchers have also found evidence that some young women perceive engineering not just as male-dominated, but as gender-biased. Studies summarized in the 2018 review found experimental evidence that women react negatively to fields in which they perceive bias and survey evidence indicating that college undergraduates, while not averse to STEM majors as a whole, perceived specific STEM fields (including engineering) as biased and were likely to avoid majoring in those fields for that reason.[lvi]

Other research suggests that this perception is not simply an invention — considerable evidence exists that engineering can be an unwelcoming field to women who seek to enter. Studies of this problem have focused on two questions: a. Do female engineers face bias in hiring and promotion decisions and b. Is there a "chilly climate" for women in engineering workplaces?

Whether there is bias in personnel decisions has become the subject of much controversy. Research conducted by Ceci and Williams (2014) contended that there is little evidence that women face employment discrimination in math-intensive STEM fields in universities. According to this research team, female candidates are at least as likely as males to interview for tenure-track positions; they also found that reviewing for grant funding and manuscript submission are gender-neutral.[lvii] These findings attracted substantial public attention as a result of an op-ed the authors wrote in *The New York Times* summarizing their research and a vigorous response in the same newspaper from critics.[lviii]

Subsequent research continues to be divided on the issue of whether discrimination exists in engineering employment. A 2017 study of actual job interviews suggested that simply examining who gets interviewed is not enough; it found evidence that female job candidates who made it through to the interview stage faced different, and more intense kinds of scrutiny than male candidates for the same positions.[lix] Research discussed in the 2020 literature review presented conflicting findings. On the one hand, one study found evidence that female doctoral recipients in several fields, including engineering, were more likely than male doctoral recipients to receive no job offer after completing their degree. Experimental research using matched resumés for male and female candidates found evidence of implicit bias in male-dominated physics, but not in more gender-integrated biology (suggesting something similar may be the case in engineering). However, a study of university faculty found that engineering faculty, in particular, when asked to recommend colleagues for various roles, were *more* likely to recommend female candidates for leadership and research roles. The study's authors speculated that this may reflect a degree of "bias correction" in a male-dominated field.[lx]

All of this research focuses on academic employment, but a study published in 2021 suggests that, outside the academy, hiring and promotion decisions may be shaped by the interaction of women's choices and implicit biases. Campero (2021) analyzed data from a hiring platform to examine the development of gender segregation in software engineering and development. He found that women are more prevalent in lower-paid, lower-status quality assurance positions in the field. This was largely the result of women's being more likely than men to apply for these positions; but, employer bias also played a role, in the sense that people employed in quality assurance roles were less likely to be considered subsequently for better-paid roles in other areas.[lxi]

The perception that employed female engineers confront a "chilly climate" in their workplaces has also been the subject of much discussion in recent years. The SWE Literature Review has discussed the growing number of published accounts of what it is like to be a woman employed in a high-tech firm. The picture that emerges is one of a "bro culture" in which sexist behavior is tolerated and in which women are subjected to a variety of indignities, microaggressions, and unequal treatment.

Lacking detailed studies of other engineering workplaces, it is impossible to say whether the conditions in the tech industry are characteristic of other engineering workplaces. However, there are at least some indications that women encounter microaggressions and sexism in a variety of engineering employment settings. We have already discussed Seron's study of the internship and work team experiences of engineering students. Research on teams in engineering has been reviewed on numerous occasions in the pages of the literature review, consistently finding that women are not treated equally when they find themselves on teams dominated by men. Research reviewed this year leads to similar conclusions. For example, Tomko et al.'s (2021) study of university maker spaces finds that female students encounter obstacles to entry and are treated as "helpless" females by their male counterparts.[lxii] Beddoes' (2021) study, based on interviews with a small number of newly hired female civil engineers, finds that they identify a variety of forms of male privilege in their workplaces, notably being taken seriously, not being subject to sexual harassment, and feeling welcomed.[lxiii]

Developing strategies to address the kinds of institutional and cultural problems these studies investigate is obviously challenging. Complicating the problem is the reality that many people, both men and women, don't acknowledge that there are structural problems involved.

Although, as some critics of NSF ADVANCE have noted, women are often cast in the role of change-maker in programs designed to modify institutional cultures; researchers have found that many female engineers are reluctant to say that sexism and bias are more than an individual matter. One of the first studies along these lines discussed in the literature review was Britton's (2017) analysis of a set of interviews with about 100 female STEM faculty at public research universities. Her respondents reported incidents of unfair and unequal treatment at work, but they did not describe them as part of a broader "chilly climate." Instead, perhaps concerned that to do so would draw additional

attention to their gender and worsen the situation, they preferred to treat these incidents as isolated cases of individual misbehavior.[lxiv]

Subsequent research confirms this finding. Seron's (2018) study of undergraduate students emphasized their resistance to identifying themselves as a "feminist." While acknowledging their marginalization as women in a male-dominated field, they attributed their success to individual effort and accepted the prevailing meritocratic interpretation of the field. To them, improving women's situation in engineering was not a matter of structural changes but of strengthening individual women's skills so that they could more effectively compete in a field they saw as largely gender-blind.[lxv] A number of studies summarized in the 2019 review painted a similar picture of the attitudes of female engineers and scientists, which one referred to as "STEMinism."[lxvi]

Research published in 2021 continued along the same lines. The eight women who held engineering leadership positions in Germany studied by Schmitt (2021) believed that succeeding in the profession required adapting to the male "habitus" of engineering. Although conscious of gender inequality in the profession, all reported trying to stay invisible as women in order to maintain their identity as an engineer.[lxvii] Somewhat more encouragingly for advocates of institutional transformation, Bird and Rhoton's (2021) study of a group of faculty involved with NSF ADVANCE found that there was a range of opinions among their respondents about whether STEM disciplines were meritocratic; faculty in departments in which women were in a significant minority (such as engineering) were *more* likely to see systematic problems. Bird and Rhoton speculate that the fact that these were ADVANCE institutions may have increased faculty members' awareness of institutionalized inequalities.[lxviii]

Studies such as these indicate that institutional transformation requires that female engineers be persuaded that it is actually necessary. Researchers also have argued that it is important to persuade men, since it is their attitudes and behaviors, and the structures they have built around them, that need to be transformed. And, male scientists and engineers, like their female colleagues, tend to see their disciplines as gender-blind, as Sattari and Sandefur's (2019) study of male STEM faculty indicated.[lxix] Even sympathetic male colleagues may see men playing a relatively limited role in institutional change. The same study found that leaders (largely male) expected men to make largely attitudinal changes ("be more sensitive") while they expected women to change more fundamentally (be more aggressive, reconsider family commitments). It is worth adding that even the expectation that women should be more aggressive is not really a commitment to *institutional* change. As a recent study of the concept of implicit bias and its role in NSF ADVANCE has noted, while it is important and useful to press for change in the attitudes of individual members of an organization, doing so does not affect the structures surrounding those individuals and may render the attitudinal changes ineffective.[lxx]

Last year's SWE Literature Review highlighted a recent book by David G. Smith and W. Brad Johnson entitled *Good Guys: How Men Can Be Better Allies for Women in the Workplace.* The book makes a strong case that men need to be part of the solution to the problem of institutional gender bias in the workplace and identifies a number of concrete ways in which they can help. However, as SWE's summary observed, the likelihood of men's play-

ing a leading role is limited by the fact, discussed above, that many men (and women) don't perceive their institutions as sexist and by the reality that many men may see women's gain as their loss.[lxxi]

## CONCLUSION

Achieving equity in occupations dominated by one sex is difficult. As the classic analysis of the issue by Barbara Reskin and Patricia Roos demonstrated years ago, it is extremely rare to find an occupation in the United States in which men and women work alongside one another in equal numbers performing the same tasks.[lxxii] We should, therefore, be impressed that women have made the significant strides in engineering the data presented at the beginning of this review document. At the same time, it is reasonable to ask whether ongoing efforts to integrate the profession further are likely to succeed and what, if anything, could be changed to make those efforts more effective.

The research summarized in the SWE Literature Review explores both the various reasons for the small numbers of women in engineering and the programs designed to increase those numbers. So, a reasonable question to ask is whether those programs are well-matched to what has been learned about the causes of gender inequities in the profession. In some cases, it is probably necessary

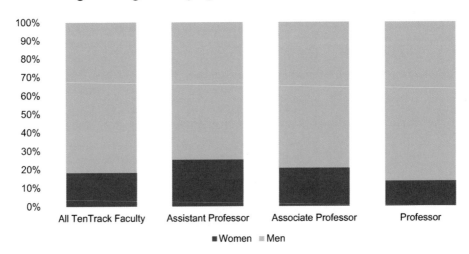

**Engineering Faculty by Rank and Percent Gender, 2020**

(Source: ASEE (2021) Profiles of Engineering and Engineering Technology. Washington DC)

to answer no. An obvious example is the ongoing emphasis on programs to improve girls' math skills and self-confidence and to improve the retention of women in engineering at the college level. As discussed earlier, the evidence suggests that there are already more than enough girls with the math skills needed to succeed in an engineering program. And, research has shown that improving girls' confidence in math alone does not make them as likely as comparable boys to aspire to an engineering career. So, while these programs are unlikely to do any harm, they also are unlikely, by themselves, to have a major impact on the gender composition of engineering.

A similar critique can be made of programs focused on improving the retention of women in college-level engineering programs. Although far from a consensus, there is a significant amount of research that challenges the view that women leave engineering degree programs in larger percentages than men. Thus, programs focused on post-secondary retention, while not harmful, likely will have only a limited impact on the numbers of women in engineering. Instead, emphasis should be placed more on making engineering more attractive to pre-college women (since decisions to enter the field occur early) and on retaining women

*after* they graduate, since there is clear evidence that female engineering graduates leave the profession at higher rates than men.

To pursue this last point somewhat further, we continue to know too little about women's experiences as working engineers and about why they leave the profession after graduating. It is clearly difficult for researchers to gain access to workplaces outside the academy. The result is that we have only a limited understanding of the role played in women's departure by the various causes researchers have suggested: work/family conflict, a chilly climate, lack of opportunities for personal development, etc. In an ideal world, a program similar to NSF-ADVANCE, that emphasized research-based, sustained institutional transformation, focused on industry could be created both to improve our understanding of women's employment experiences and match programming to what is learned.

Many of the programs described and assessed in the literature on women in engineering are relatively small-scale, short-term programs — recruitment workshops, research experiences, summer camps, etc. While these programs are well-intended, and often can show positive outcomes, the SWE Literature Review has asked

## Engineering Faculty by Rank and Percent Gender, 2002

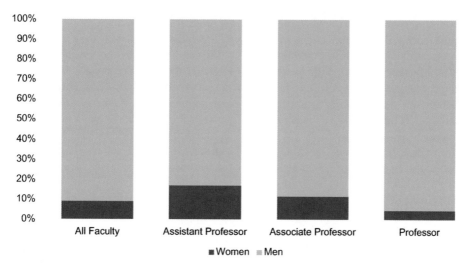

(Source: Gibbons (2003) Engineering on the Rise. ASEE. Washington DC)

on more than one occasion whether they are likely to have a lasting impact. A passage from the 2005 literature review describes the problem well:

> "Simple one-shot exposure and interest in engineering careers is probably not enough to get more girls involved in engineering programs. If that were true, then we would expect to see young female fans of 'Star Trek Voyager,' with its strong female engineering characters, flocking to the field." (p. 64)

So, perhaps more broadly based, regional or national efforts to attract more women to engineering are needed. And, it is worth adding that those efforts should target not just middle- and high-school students but also include the goal of developing alternative pipelines to engineering. In last year's review, we summarized interesting research showing that some women develop an interest in engineering once they have already completed their college education, but returning to complete a second degree is often impractical because of the amount of time and money required. Two-year colleges also are a potential recruiting site for students, especially students of color, but the path from a two-year program to a four-year engineering program is often discouragingly complex.[lxxiii] Finding ways to make it possible for nontraditional students to complete engineering programs would help expand the pool of women from which the profession could recruit. An interesting option that might help solve this problem was described in the 2011 review; the DEEP (Deconstructing Engineering Education Programs) project demonstrated the possibility of simplifying the engineering curriculum by drastically reducing the length of prerequisite strings.[lxxiv] Of course, achieving this kind of curricular reform is very difficult and likely to require considerable amounts of time.

It is possible to be optimistic that the United States will be a leader in achieving gender equity in engineering and that the kinds of programs that are needed to achieve it will be developed relatively soon. After all, the U.S. has a relatively egalitarian culture in which, in theory at least, ideas about gender equity should thrive. However, researchers have argued that even relatively egalitarian cultures can harbor persistent ideas about gender difference. Charles and Bradley's seminal analysis of sex segregation in higher education found that "universalistic" norms undermine vertical segregation (i.e., norms about who can participate in various levels of education) much more rapidly than horizonal segregation (which fields of study are appropriate for men or women).[lxxv] Although there is evidence that, in more egalitarian countries, the gender gap in science career expectations is smaller,[lxxvi] research also has shown that, in those countries, women who have high science and math scores typically *also* have high verbal scores — indeed their verbal scores are often their best test results. So, compared with men who have high science and math scores, these women have more options and may choose careers outside engineering or science or careers in science where women are more common, such as health care careers.[lxxvii]

An interesting article published in 2021 describes one way in which girls who are strong in science and math are sometimes drawn away from careers such as engineering. Pitt, Brockman, and Zhu (2021)[lxxviii] analyze data on a sample of students who double-majored in college. They found that women were more likely than men to select a non-STEM major as their second major and to express dissatisfaction with their STEM major. Although they had been pushed by parents and others to select a STEM major, these double majors often expressed more "love" for their (non-STEM) second major, a fact that suggests they may be drawn toward non-STEM careers or would be more likely to abandon a STEM career after having begun it.

We are thus led back to the question of making engineering more attractive. If women are choosing other options they see as more inviting, how can engineering be made to seem a better choice? As we've seen, this is not just a matter of talking about engineering's virtues. If the field is perceived as hostile to women, and if women's experiences in the field bear that out, they are unlikely to select it from the available options or to stay if they begin an engineering career. Thus, the focus needs to be on men, as well as women. In addition to persuading women that engineering is something they can do and will enjoy, men must be persuaded to support their efforts and to change a culture that too often is unwelcoming to its female recruits. ✿

## About the authors

*Peter Meiksins, Ph.D., is Professor Emeritus of Sociology at Cleveland State University. He received his B.A. from Columbia University and Ph.D. from York University, Toronto. Major publications include* Putting Work in Its Place: A Quiet Revolution, *with Peter Whalley, Ph.D. (2002), and* Changing Contours of Work: Jobs and Opportunities in the New Economy, *4th edition, with Stephen Sweet, Ph.D. (2020).*

*Peggy Layne, P.E., F.SWE, is former assistant provost and director of the ADVANCE program at Virginia Tech. She holds degrees in environmental and water resources engineering and science and technology studies. Layne is the editor of* Women in Engineering: Pioneers and Trailblazers *and* Women in Engineering: Professional Life *(ASCE Press, 2009). A Fellow of the Society of Women Engineers, Layne served as SWE FY97 president.*

## Endnotes

i Frehill, L. (2004). The Gendered Construction of the Engineering Profession in the United States, 1893-1920. *Men and Masculinities* 6(4): 383-403.

ii Hacker, S. (1990) Mathematization of Engineering: Limits on Women and the Field, pp. 139–154 in Dorothy E. Smith and Susan M. Turner (eds) *Doing it the Hard Way: Investigations of Gender and Technology*. London: Unwin Hyman.

iii See the 2005 SWE Literature Review, pp. 60-61.

iv Ceci, S.J., Williams, W.M., and Barnett, S.M. (2009). Women's Underrepresentation in Science: Sociocultural and Biological Considerations. *Psychological Bulletin* 135(2): 218-261.

v Cimpian, J.R., Kim, T.H., and McDermott, Z.T. (2020). Understanding Persistent Gender Gaps in STEM. *Science* 368(6497): 1317-1319.

vi Kimmel, L.G., Miller, J.D., and Eccles, J.S. (2012). Do the Paths to STEMM Professions Differ by Gender? *Peabody Journal of Education* (0161956X) 87(1): 92-113.

vii Valla, J.M. and Ceci, S.J. (2014). Breadth-Based Models of Women's Underrepresentation in STEM Fields: An Integrative Commentary on Schmidt (2011) and Nye et al. (2012). *Perspectives on Psychological Science* 9(2): 219–224.

viii For an example, see Seo, E., Shen, Y., and Alfaro, E.C. (2019). Adolescents' Beliefs About Math Ability and Their Relations to STEM Career Attainment: Joint Consideration of Race/Ethnicity and Gender. *Journal of Youth & Adolescence* 48(2): 306–325.

ix Riegle-Crumb, C. and Peng, M. (2021). Examining High School Students' Gendered Beliefs about Math: Predictors and Implications for Choice of STEM College Majors. *Sociology of Education* 94(3): 227-48.

x SWE Magazine Review of the Literature (2001): summary of argument made in Isaacs, B. (2001). Mystery of the Missing Women Engineers: A Solution. *Journal of Professional Issues in Engineering Education and Practice* 127(2): 85-91.

xi Cross, K.J. et al. (2021). The Pieces of Me: The Double Bind of Race and Gender in Engineering. *Journal of Women and Minorities in Science and Engineering* 27(3): 79-105.

xii True-Funk, A. et al. (2021). Intersectional Engineers: Diversity of Gender and Race Microaggressions and Their Effects in Engineering Education. *Journal of Management in Engineering* 37(3).

xiii Ross, M., Huff, J.L., and Godwin, A. (2021). Resilient Engineering Identity Development Critical to Prolonged Engagement of Black Women in Engineering. *Journal of Engineering Education* 110(1): 92-113.

xiv See the 2013 SWE Literature Review, pp. 246-8 for a more detailed review of the findings summarized here.

xv Yang, J.A. et al. (2021). Resistance and Community-building in LGBTQ+ Engineering Students. *Journal of Women and Minorities in Science and Engineering* 27(4): 1-33.

# Women Deans of Engineering Then and Now

## 2001

**Eleanor Baum, Ph.D.**
Dean, Cooper Union

**Cynthia S. Hirtzel, Ph.D.**
Dean, Youngstown State University

**Denice D. Denton, Ph.D.**
Dean, University of Washington

**Ilene Busch-Vishniac, Ph.D.**
Dean, Johns Hopkins University

**Nancy Jannik, Ph.D.**
Dean, Winona State University

**Janie Fouke, Ph.D.**
Dean, Michigan State University

**Mary L. Good, Ph.D.**
Dean, University of Arkansas, Little Rock

**Kristina M. Johnson, Ph.D.**
Dean, Duke University

**Sandra J. DeLoatch, Ph.D.**
Dean, Norfolk State University

**Dianne Dorland, Ph.D.**
Dean, Rowan University

**Linda C. Lucas, Ph.D.**
Dean, The University of Alabama at Birmingham

**Zorica Pantić, Ph.D.**
Dean, The University of Texas at San Antonio

**Diane Schwartz, Ph.D.**
Interim Dean, California State University, Northridge

## AS OF 2020 AND 2021

**Cammy R. Abernathy, Ph.D.**
Dean, University of Florida

**Alexis R. Abramson, Ph.D.**
Dean, Dartmouth College

**Stephanie G. Adams, Ph.D.**
Dean and Lars Magnus Ericsson Chair, The University of Texas at Dallas

**Nancy Allbritton, Ph.D.**
Dean, University of Washington

**Emily L. Allen, Ph.D.**
Dean, California State University, Los Angeles

**Sara A. Atwood, Ph.D.**
Dean, Elizabethtown College

**M. Katherine Banks, Ph.D.**
Vice Chancellor and Dean of Engineering, Texas A&M University

**Gilda A. Barabino, Ph.D.**
President, Olin College of Engineering

**Susamma Barua, Ph.D.**
Dean, California State University, Fullerton

**Alison A. Baski, Ph.D.**
Dean, College of Science, California State Polytechnic University, Pomona

**Stella N. Batalama, Ph.D.**
Dean, Florida Atlantic University

**Gail Baura, Ph.D.**
Director, Loyola University Chicago

**Joanne M. Belovich, Ph.D.**
Interim Dean, Cleveland State University

**Barbara D. Boyan, Ph.D.**
Dean, Virginia Commonwealth University

**Mary C. Boyce, Ph.D.**
Dean, Columbia University

**Bethany Brinkman, Ph.D., P.E.**
Director, Sweet Briar College

**JoAnn Browning, Ph.D., P.E.**
Dean, The University of Texas at San Antonio

**Lynn K. Byers, P.E.**
Interim Dean, Quinnipiac University

**Janet Callahan, Ph.D.**
Dean, Michigan Technological University

**Naira H. Campbell-Kyureghyan, Ph.D.**
Dean, Merrimack College

**Jenna P. Carpenter, Ph.D.**
Dean, Campbell University

**Judy L. Cezeaux, Ph.D.**
Dean, Arkansas Tech University

**Tina Choe, Ph.D.**
Dean, Loyola Marymount University

**Robin Coger, Ph.D.**
Dean, North Carolina A&T University

**Leslie Cornick, Ph.D.**
Dean, University of Washington Bothell

**Patricia J. Culligan, Ph.D.**
Dean, University of Notre Dame

**Jennifer Sinclair Curtis, Ph.D.**
Dean, University of California, Davis

**Doreen Edwards, Ph.D.**
Dean, Rochester Institute of Technology

**Sheryl H. Ehrman, Ph.D.**
Dean, San Jose State University

**Stephanie Farrell, Ph.D.**
Interim Dean, Rowan University

**Amy S. Fleischer, Ph.D.**
Dean, California Polytechnic State University, San Luis Obispo

**Kimberly Foster, Ph.D.**
Dean, Tulane University

**Marcia Friesen, P.Eng.**
Dean, Faculty of Engineering, University of Manitoba

**Claire Fuller, Ph.D.**
Dean, Murray State University

**Gabrielle Gaustad, Ph.D.**
Dean, Alfred University

**Andrea J. Goldsmith, Ph.D.**
Dean, Princeton University

**Molly M. Gribb, Ph.D., P.E.**
Dean, University of Wisconsin-Platteville

**Cyndee Gruden, Ph.D.**
Dean, University of New Hampshire

**Christine Hailey, Ph.D.**
Dean, Texas State University, San Marcos

**Angela Hare, Ph.D.**
Dean, Messiah College

**Wendi Beth Heinzelman, Ph.D.**
Dean, University of Rochester

**Karlene A. Hoo, Ph.D.**
Dean, Gonzaga University

**Ayanna Howard, Ph.D.**
Dean, The Ohio State University

**Emily M. Hunt, Ph.D.**
Dean, West Texas A&M University

**Jacqueline A. Isaacs, Ph.D.**
Interim Dean, Northeastern University

**Erin Jablonski, Ph.D.**
Interim Dean, Bucknell University

Brig. Gen. Cindy Jebb, Ph.D.
Dean, Academic Board, U.S. Military Academy

Maria V. Kalevitch, Ph.D.
Dean, Robert Morris University

Jelena Kovačević, Ph.D.
Dean, New York University

Hyun J. Kwon, Ph.D.
Chair, Engineering and Computer Science, Andrews University

Laura W. Lackey, Ph.D., P.E.
Dean, Mercer University

Nancy K. Lape, Ph.D.
Interim Chair of Engineering, Harvey Mudd College

JoAnn S. Lighty, Ph.D.
Dean, Boise State University

Tsu-Jae King Liu, Ph.D.
Dean, University of California, Berkeley

Tracy Bradley Maples, Ph.D.
Interim Dean, California State University, Long Beach

Michele S. Marcolongo, Ph.D.
Dean, Villanova University

Denise M. Martinez, Ph.D.
Associate Dean, Tarleton State University

Patricia F. Mead, Ph.D.
Department Chair, Norfolk State University

Charla Miertschin, Ph.D.
Dean, Winona State University

Lynne A. Molter, Sc.D.
Interim Chair, Swarthmore College

Kimberly Muller, Ph.D.
Dean, College of Innovation and Solutions, Lake Superior State University

Jayathi Y. Murthy, Ph.D.
Dean, University of California, Los Angeles

Kim LaScola Needy, Ph.D., P.E.
Dean, University of Arkansas

Harriet B. Nembhard, Ph.D.
Dean, The University of Iowa

Pamela Holland Obiomon, Ph.D.
Dean, Prairie View A&M University

Elizabeth Jane Orwin, Ph.D.
Chair, Harvey Mudd College

Margaret Pinnell, Ph.D.
Interim Dean, University of Dayton

Wendy Reed, Ph.D.
Dean, University of Minnesota Duluth

Mary Rezac, Ph.D.
Dean, Washington State University

Jinny Rhee, Ph.D.
Dean, California State University, Long Beach

Kristina M. Ropella, Ph.D.
Dean, Marquette University

Julia M. Ross, Ph.D.
Dean, Virginia Tech

Michelle B. Sabick, Ph.D.
Dean, Saint Louis University

Anca L. Sala, Ph.D.
Dean, Baker College

Linda S. Schadler, Ph.D.
Dean, The University of Vermont

Elaine P. Scott, Ph.D.
Dean, Santa Clara University

Ying Shang, Ph.D.
Dean, University of Evansville

Joyce T. Shirazi, Ph.D.
Dean, Hampton University

Katherine Snyder, Ph.D.
Dean, University of Detroit Mercy

Beena Sukumaran, Ph.D.
Dean, Miami University (Ohio)

Janis P. Terpenny, Ph.D.
Wayne T. Davis Chair of Engineering and Dean, The University of Tennessee

Jean S. VanderGheynst, Ph.D.
Dean, University of Massachusetts Dartmouth

Karinna M. Vernaza, Ph.D.
Dean, Gannon University

Sharon Walker, Ph.D.
Dean, Drexel University

Mary Wells, Ph.D., P.Eng.
Dean, Faculty of Engineering, University of Waterloo

Jennifer L. West, Ph.D.
Dean, University of Virginia

Jennifer Widom, Ph.D.
Dean, Stanford University

Stacy S. Wilson, Ph.D.
Director, Western Kentucky University

Sharon L. Wood, Ph.D., P.E.
Dean, The University of Texas at Austin

Judy Wornat, Ph.D.
Dean, Louisiana State University

Yan Xiang, Ph.D.
Dean, Southern New Hampshire University

Sharon Zelmanowitz, Ph.D., P.E.
Department Head, Engineering, U.S. Coast Guard Academy

Jean Zu, Ph.D., P.Eng.
Dean, Stevens Institute of Technology

---

*Note: Because some schools' engineering programs consist of only one or a small number of departments rather than a college or a school, their leaders may have titles such as director or chair rather than dean. Definitions and terminology can vary from institution to institution.*

xvi Alfrey, L. and Winddance Twine, F. (2017). Gender-Fluid Geek Girls: Negotiating Inequality Regimes in the Tech Industry. *Gender and Society* 31(1): 28–50.

xvii Holian, L. and Kelly, E. (2020). STEM Occupational Intentions: Stability and Change Through High School. Stats in Brief. NCES 2020-167. National Center for Education Statistics.

xviii For example, this is the case for a major research project funded by NSF at the University of Wisconsin-Milwaukee. See Fouad, N.A., Singh, R., Cappaert, K., Chang, W., and Wan, M. (2016). Comparison of Women Engineers Who Persist in or Depart from Engineering. *Journal of Vocational Behavior* 92: 79–93.

xix Frehill, L. (2010). Satisfaction. *Mechanical Engineering* 132(1): 38-41.

xx Cheryan, S., Ziegler, S., Montoya, A., and Jiang, L. (2016). Why Are Some STEM Fields More Gender Balanced than Others? *Psychological Bulletin*, October.

xxi Denice, P. (2021). Choosing and Changing Course: Postsecondary Students and the Process of Selecting a Major Field of Study. *Sociological Perspectives* 64(1): 82-108.

xxii Preston, A. (2004). *Leaving Science: Occupational Exit from Scientific Careers Between 1965 and 1995*. NY: Russell Sage Foundation.

xxiii Singh, R., Zhang, Y., Wan, M. (Maggie), and Fouad, N.A. (2018). Why Do Women Engineers Leave the Engineering Profession? The Roles of Work-Family Conflict, Occupational Commitment, and Perceived Organizational Support. *Human Resource Management* 57(4): 901–914; Cech, E.A. and Blair-Loy, M. (2019). The Changing Career Trajectories of New Parents in STEM. *PNAS* 116(10): 4182–4187.

xxiv Ecklund, E.H. and Lincoln, A.E. (2016). *Failing Families, Failing Science: Work-Family Conflict in Academic Science*. New York: New York University Press.

xxv Holmes, M. (2016). Why Women Leave Engineering: The SWE Gender Culture Study. *SWE Magazine* 62(2): 10-12.

xxvi Fouad, N.A., Singh, R., Cappaert, K., Chang, W., and Wan, M. (2016), op. cit.

xxvii Thébaud, S. and Taylor, C.J. (2021). The Specter of Motherhood: Culture and the Production of Gendered Career Aspirations in Science and Engineering. *Gender and Society* 35(3): 395-421.

xxviii Seron, C., Silbey, S.S., Cech, E., and Rubineau, B. (2016). Persistence Is Cultural: Professional Socialization and the Reproduction of Sex Segregation. *Work and Occupations* 43(2): 178–214.

xxix Wynn, A.T. and Correll, S.J. (2018). Puncturing the Pipeline: Do Technology Companies Alienate Women in Recruiting Sessions? *Social Studies of Science* 48(1): 149-164.

xxx See 2006 SWE Literature Review, pp. 91-93 for a summary of these early assessments.

xxxi Bilimoria, D. and Buch, K.K. (2010). The Search Is On: Engendering Faculty Diversity Through More Effective Search and Recruitment. *Change* 42(4): 27-32.

xxxii Bilimoria, D. and Liang, X. (2012). *Gender Equity in Science and Engineering: Advancing Change in Higher Education*. New York: Routledge.

xxxiii Nelson, L. and Zippel, K. (2021). From Theory to Practice and Back: How the Concept of Implicit Bias Was Implemented in Academe and What This Means for Theories of Organizational Change. *Gender and Society* 35(3): 330-357.

xxxiv Morimoto, S.A. and Zajicek, A. (2014). Dismantling the "Master's House": Feminist Reflections on Institutional Transformation. *Critical Sociology* 40(1): 135-150.

xxxv Zippel, K. and Ferree, M.M. (2019). Organizational Interventions and the Creation of Gendered Knowledge: US Universities and NSF ADVANCE. *Gender, Work and Organization* 26(6): 805–821.

xxxvi Mack, P.E. (2001). What Difference Has Feminism Made to Engineering in the Twentieth Century? p. 149-68 in Creager, A., Lunbeck, E., and Schiebinger, L. (eds), *Feminism in Twentieth Century Science, Technology and Medicine*. Chicago: University of Chicago Press.

xxxvii Salas-Morera, L. et al. (2021). Understanding Why Women Don't Choose Engineering Degrees. *International Journal of Technology and Design Education* 31: 325-338.

xxxviii See, for example, Shi, Y. (2018). The Puzzle of Missing Female Engineers: Academic Preparation, Ability Beliefs, and Preferences. *Economics of Education Review* 64(C): 129-143.

xxxix Cheryan, S., Ziegler, S., Montoya, A., and Jiang, L. (2016), op. cit.

xl Kelley, M.S. and Bryan, K.K. (2018). Gendered Perceptions of Typical Engineers Across Specialties for Engineering Majors. *Gender and Education* 30(1): 22–44.

xli McGuire, L., Jefferys, E., and Rutland, A. (2020). Children's Evaluations of Deviant Peers in the Context of Science and Technology: The Role of Gender Group Norms and Status. *Journal of Experimental Child Psychology* 195.

xlii Veldman, J. et al. (2021). "Where Will I Belong More?": The Role of Belonging Comparisons Between STEM Fields in High School Girls' STEM Interests. *Social Psychology of Education* 24(5): 1363-1387.

xliii Bian, L., Leslie, S.-J., and Cimpian, A. (2017). Gender Stereotypes About Intellectual Ability Emerge Early and Influence Children's Interests. *Science* 355(6323): 389–391.

xliv Su, R. and Rounds, J. (2015). All STEM Fields Are Not Created Equal: People and Things Interests Explain Gender Disparities Across STEM Fields. *Frontiers in Psychology* 6(February): 20.

xlv Cech, E. (2015). Engineers and Engineeresses? Self-Conceptions and the Development of Gendered Professional Identities. *Sociological Perspectives* 58(1): 56–77.

xlvi Patrick, A., Riegle-Crumb, C., and Borrego, M. (2021). Examining the Gender Gap in Engineering Professional Identification. *Journal of Women and Minorities in Science and Engineering* 27(1): 31-55.

xlvii See the 2019 SWE Literature Review, pp. 413 and 416.

xlviii Ertl, B. and Hartmann, F.G. (2019). The Interest Profiles and Interest Congruence of Male and Female Students in STEM and Non-STEM Fields. *Frontiers in Psychology* 10: 897.

xlix See the 2006 SWE Literature Review, pp. 81-84 and the 2008 SWE Literature Review, pp. 151-53.

l Fox, M.F., Sonnert, G., and Nikiforova, I. (2009). Successful Programs for Undergraduate Women in Science and Engineering: *Adapting* versus *Adopting* the Institutional Environment. *Research in Higher Education* 50(4): 333-353.

li Bodnar, K. et al. (2020). Science Identity Predicts Science Career Aspiration Across Gender and Race, but Especially for White Boys. *International Journal of Gender, Science and Technology* 12(1): 33-45.

lii d'Entremont, A.G., Greer, K., and Lyon, K.A. (2020). Does Adding "Helping Disciplines" to Engineering Schools Contribute to Gender Parity? 2020 ASEE Virtual Annual Conference Content Access.

liii Diekman, A.B., Steinberg, M., Brown, E.R., Belanger, A.L., and Clark, E.K. (2017). A Goal Congruity Model of Role Entry, Engagement, and Exit: Understanding Communal Goal Processes in STEM Gender Gaps. Personality and Social Psychology Review (Sage Publications Inc.) 21(2): 142–175.

liv Smith-Doerr, L., Vardi, I., and Croissant, J. (2016). Doing Gender and Responsibility: Scientists and Engineers Talk about Their Work. *Journal of Women and Minorities in Science and Engineering* 22(1): 49–68.

lv Pearlman, J. (2019). Occupational Mobility for Whom?: Education, Cohorts, the Life Course and Occupational Gender Composition, 1970–2010. *Research in Social Stratification and Mobility* 59: 81–93.

lvi Moss-Racusin, C.A., Sanzari, C., Caluori, N., and Rabasco, H. (2018). Gender Bias Produces Gender Gaps in STEM Engagement. *Sex Roles* 79(11-12): 651-670; Ganley, C.M., George, C.E., Cimpian, J.R., and Makowski, M.B. (2018). Gender Equity in College Majors: Looking Beyond the STEM/Non-STEM Dichotomy for Answers Regarding Female Participation. *American Educational Research Journal* 55(3): 453–487.

lvii Ceci, S., Ginther, D., Kahn, S., and Williams, W. (2014). Women in Academic Science: A Changing Landscape. *Psychological Science in the Public Interest* 15(3): 75–141.

lviii See the 2014 SWE Literature Review, pp. 266-71 for a summary of the controversy.

lix Blair-Loy, M., Rogers, L.E., Glaser, D., Wong, Y.L. Anne, Abraham, D., and Cosman, P.C. (2017). Gender in Engineering Departments: Are There Gender Differences in Interruptions of Academic Job Talks? *Social Sciences* 6(1): 29.

lx Kinoshita, T.J., Knight, D.B., Borrego, M., and Wall Bortz, W.E. (2020). Illuminating Systematic Differences in No Job Offers for STEM Doctoral Recipients. *PLOS ONE* 15(4): 1–23; Eaton, A.A., Saunders, J.F., Jacobson, R.K., and West, K. (2020). How Gender and Race Stereotypes Impact the Advancement of Scholars in STEM: Professors' Biased Evaluations of Physics and Biology Post-Doctoral Candidates. *Sex Roles* 82(3/4): 127–141; Judson, E., Ross, L., Krause, S.J., Hjelmstad, K.D., and Mayled, L.H. (2020). How a STEM Faculty Member's Gender Affects Career Guidance from Others: Comparing Engineering to Biology and Physics. 2020 ASEE Virtual Annual Conference Content Access.

lxi Campero, S. (2021). Hiring and Intra-Occupational Gender Segregation in Software Engineering. *American Sociological Review.* 86(1): 60-92.

lxii Tomko, M. et al. (2021). Participation Pathways for Women into University Makerspaces. *Journal of Engineering Education* 110:700-17.

lxiii Beddoes, K. (2021). Examining Privilege in Engineering Socialization Through the Stories of Newcomer Engineers. *Engineering Studies* 13(2):158-179.

lxiv Britton, D.M. (2017). Beyond the Chilly Climate: The Salience of Gender in Women's Academic Careers. *Gender and Society* 31(1): 5-27.

lxv Seron, C. Silbey, S., Cech, E., and Rubineau, B. (2018). "I Am Not a Feminist, but. . .": Hegemony of a Meritocratic Ideology and the Limits of Critique Among Women in Engineering. *Work and Occupations* 45(2): 131–167.

lxvi See the 2019 SWE Literature Review, p. 437 for a summary of these studies. The term STEMinism comes from Myers, K., C. Gallaher, and S. McCarragher (2019). STEMinism. *Journal of Gender Studies* 28(6): 648–660.

lxvii Schmitt, M. (2021). Women Engineers on Their Way to Leadership: The Role of Social Support Within Engineering Work Cultures. *Engineering Studies* 13(1): 30-52.

lxviii Bird, S.R. and Rhoton, L.A. (2021). Seeing Isn't Always Believing: Gender, Academic STEM, and Women Scientists' Perceptions of Career Opportunities. *Gender and Society* 35(3): 422-448.

lxix Sattari, N. and Sandefur, R.L. (2019). Gender in Academic STEM: A Focus on Men Faculty. *Gender, Work and Organization* 26(2): 158–179.

lxx Nelson, A. and Zippel, K. (2021), op. cit.

lxxi Smith, D.G. and Johnson, W.B. (2020). *Good Guys: How Men Can Be Better Allies for Women in the Workplace.* Boston: Harvard Business Review Press. See 2020 SWE Literature Review, pp. 458-59 for a review of this book.

lxxii Reskin, B. and P. Roos (1990). *Job Queues, Gender Queues: Explaining Women's Inroads into Male Occupations.* Philadelphia: Temple University Press.

lxxiii See the 2020 SWE Literature Review, pp. 478-9 for a more detailed statement of these arguments and references to the relevant literature.

lxxiv Busch-Vishniac, I., Kibler, T., Campbell, P., Patterson, E., Guillaume, D., Jarosz, J., Chassapis, C., Emery, A., Ellis, G., Whitworth, H., Metz, S., Brainard, S., and Ray, P. (2011). Deconstructing Engineering Education Programmes: The DEEP Project to Reform the Mechanical

Engineering Curriculum. *European Journal of Engineering Education* 36(3): 269-283.

lxxv Charles, M. and Bradley, K. (2002). Equal but Separate? A Cross-National Study of Sex Segregation in Higher Education. *American Sociological Review* 67(4): 573-599.

lxxvi McDaniel, A. (2016). The Role of Cultural Contexts in Explaining Cross-National Gender Gaps in STEM Expectations. *European Sociological Review* 32(1): 122-133.

lxxvii *Psychological Science* (0956-7976) 29(4): 581-593.

lxxviii Pitt, R.N., Brockman, A., and Zhu, L. (2021). Parental Pressure and Passion: Competing Motivations for Choosing STEM and Non-STEM Majors Among Women Who Double-Major in Both. *Journal of Women and Minorities in Science and Engineering* 27(1): 1-29.

*Note: An extensive bibliography of the 2021 literature follows.*

## 2021 Bibliography

Abdulina, N., Abisheva, A., Movchun, V., Lobuteva, A., and Lobuteva, L. (2021). Overcoming Gender Stereotypes in the Process of Social Development and Getting Higher Education in Digital Environment. *International Journal of Emerging Technologies in Learning* 16(12): 36–50.

Abdullah, O., Kamaludin, A., and Rahman, N.S.A. (2021). Gender Differences in Computational Thinking Skills Among Malaysian's Primary School Students Using Visual Programming. 7th International Conference on Software Engineering and Computer Systems and 4th International Conference on Computational Science and Information Management, ICSECS-ICOCSIM 2021, Aug. 24-26, 655–660.

Akinlolu, M. and Haupt, T.C. (2021). Gender and Career Choice Behaviour: Social Cognitive Predictors of Persistence in Construction Education. 14th Built Environment Conference on Association of Schools of Construction of Southern Africa, ASOCSA 2020, Sept. 21-22, 654(1).

Almeida, J. and Daniel, A.D. (2021). Women in Engineering: Developing Entrepreneurial Intention Through Learning by Doing Approach. 2021 IEEE Global Engineering Education Conference, EDUCON 2021, April 21-23, 116–121.

Alonso-Virgós, L., Fondon, M.D., Espada, J.P., and Crespo, R.G. (2021). Women in Science and Technology Studies: A Study About the Influence of Parents on Their Children's Choice of Speciality and About the Trend of the Different Specialities in Spanish Students. 2021 IEEE Global Engineering Education Conference, EDUCON 2021, April 21-23, 122–130.

Alzayed, M.A. and Miller, S.R. (2021). Factors Influencing Undergraduates' Selection of an Engineering Discipline: A Case Study. *International Journal of Engineering Education* 37(2): 482–496.

Ashlock, J., Stojnic, M., and Tufekci, Z. (2021). Gender Differences in Academic Efficacy Across STEM Fields. *Sociological Perspectives*, 1.

Axell, C. and Bostrom, J. (2021). Technology in Children's Picture Books as an Agent for Reinforcing or Challenging Traditional Gender Stereotypes. *International Journal of Technology and Design Education* 31(1): 27–39.

Ayuso, N., Fillola, E., Masia, B., Murillo, A.C., Trillo-Lado, R., Baldassarri, S., Cerezo, E., Ruberte, L., Mariscal, M.D., and Villarroya-Gaudo, M. (2021). Gender Gap in STEM: A Cross-Sectional Study of Primary School Students' Self-Perception and Test Anxiety in Mathematics. *IEEE Transactions on Education* 64(1): 40–49.

Bahnson, M., Perkins, H., Tsugawa, M., Satterfield, D., Parker, M., Cass, C., and Kirn, A. (2021). Inequity in Graduate Engineering Identity: Disciplinary Differences and Opportunity Structures. *Journal of Engineering Education* 110(4): 949–976.

Baker, N. (2021). Power Stations, Bridges and Skyscrapers: Forgotten Figures in Structural Engineering History. *Structural Engineer* 99(8): 8–13.

Beddoes, K. (2021a). Examining Privilege in Engineering Socialization Through the Stories of Newcomer Engineers. *Engineering Studies* 13(2): 158–179.

Beddoes, K. (2021b). Gender as Structure in the Organisational Socialisation of Newcomer Civil Engineers. *European Journal of Engineering Education* 47(1): 102–116.

Bencivenga, R. (2021). Transferability of Methods and Strategies for Advancing Gender Equality in Academia and Research: A Case Study of an Online Course Aimed at Academics and Professionals. 9th International Workshop on Learning Technology for Education Challenges, LTEC 2021, July 20-22, 1428: 90–100.

Bird, S.R. and Rhoton, L.A. (2021). Seeing Isn't Always Believing: Gender, Academic STEM, and Women Scientists' Perceptions of Career Opportunities. *Gender and Society* 35(3): 422–448.

Block, B.-M. and Guerne, M.G. (2021). Gender and Diversity Aspects in Engineering Education and Their Impact on the Design of Engineering Curricula. 2021 IEEE Global Engineering Education Conference, EDUCON 2021, April 21-23, 738–744.

Brigham, M. and Porquet-Lupine, J. (2021). Gender Differences in Class Participation in Core CS Courses. 26th ACM Conference on Innovation and Technology in Computer Science Education, ITiCSE 2021, June 26-July 1, 478–483.

Buckley, J., Hyland, T., Gumaelius, L., Seery, N., and Pears, A. (2021). Exploring the Prototypical Definitions of Intelligent Engineers Held by Irish and Swedish Higher Education Engineering Students. *Psychological Reports* 1.

Campbell, A.L., Direito, I., and Mokhithi, M. (2021). Developing Growth Mindsets in Engineering Students: A Systematic Literature Review of Interventions. *European Journal of Engineering Education* 46(4): 503–527.

Campero, S. (2021). Hiring and Intra-occupational Gender Segregation in Software Engineering. *American Sociological Review* 86(1): 60–92.

Cheong, M., Leins, K., and Coghlan, S. (2021). Computer Science Communities: Who Is Speaking, and Who Is Listening to the Women? Using an Ethics of Care to Promote Diverse Voices. 4th ACM Conference on Fairness, Accountability, and Transparency, FAccT 2021, March 3-10, 106–115.

Cole, K.D. (2021). To Engineer Is Human: Gender Issues in the Engineering Workplace. *Torch* 92(2): 10–14.

Cross, K.J., Mendenhall, R., Clancy, K.B.H., Imoukhuede, P., and Amos, J. (2021). The Pieces of Me: The Double Bind of Race and Gender in Engineering. *Journal of Women and Minorities in Science and Engineering* 27(3): 79–105.

Dabic, M., Vlacic, B., Obradovic, T., Marzi, G., and Kraus, S. (2021). Women in Engineering as a Research Topic: Past, Present, and Future. 2021 IEEE Technology and Engineering Management Conference - Europe, TEMSCON-EUR 2021, May 17-20, 1–6.

Denden, M., Tlili, A., Essalmi, F., Jemni, M., Chen, N.-S., and Burgos, D. (2021). Effects of Gender and Personality Differences on Students' Perception of Game Design Elements in Educational Gamification. *International Journal of Human-Computer Studies* 154(C).

Dengate, J., Farenhorst, A., Peter, T., and Franz-Odendaal, T. (2021). "Shining Armour": What Margaret-Ann Armour Taught Us About Equity, Diversity, and Inclusion and Mentorship in the Natural Sciences. *Canadian Journal of Chemistry* 99(8): 692–697.

Denice, P.A. (2021). Choosing and Changing Course: Postsecondary Students and the Process of Selecting a Major Field of Study. *Sociological Perspectives* 64(1): 82–108.

Duarte, T., Lopes, A., and da Silva, L. (2021). Correlating Entrance Data and First Year Academic Performance of Students Enrolled in the Integrated Master in Mechanical Engineering at the University of Porto. *International Journal of Mechanical Engineering Education* 1.

Felizardo, K.R., Ramos, A.M., de O. Melo, C., de Souza, E.F., Vijaykumar, N.L., and Nakagawa, E.Y. (2021). Global and Latin American Female Participation in Evidence-Based Software Engineering: A Systematic Mapping Study. *Journal of the Brazilian Computer Society* 27(1).

Females Can Break Through STEM Ceiling. (2021). *USA Today Magazine* 150(2915): 4–4.

Fernandez-de la Pena, C.P., Gomez-Aladro, V.A., Alvarez-Palacios, L., and Diaz-Tufinio, C.A. (2021). Work in Progress: Safe Environments and Female Role Models: Important Factors for Girls Approaching STEM-related Careers Through Robotics Initiatives. 2021 IEEE Global Engineering Education Conference, EDUCON 2021, April 21-23, 25–29.

Fisk, S.R., Wingate, T., Battestilli, L., and Stolee, K.T. (2021). Increasing Women's Persistence in Computer Science by Decreasing Gendered Self-Assessments of Computing Ability. 26th ACM Conference on Innovation and Technology in Computer Science Education, ITiCSE 2021, June 26-July 1, 464–470.

Forte-Celaya, M.R., Sandoval-Correa, A., Resendez-Maqueda, L.F., and Oropeza, R.S. (2021). Findings for Flexible Digital Model (MFD) Courses to Enhance Women Participation in Industrial and

Systems Engineering Courses. 2021 IEEE Global Engineering Education Conference, EDUCON 2021, April 21-23, 530–536.

Francis, V. and Michielsens, E. (2021). Exclusion and Inclusion in the Australian AEC Industry and Its Significance for Women and Their Organizations. *Journal of Management in Engineering* 37(5).

Garcia-Garcia, R.M., Gonzalez, R.S., Lara-Prieto, V., and Membrillo-Hernandez, J. (2021). Women for Leadership in Engineering: A Link Between Students and High-Impact Projects. 2021 IEEE Global Engineering Education Conference, EDUCON 2021, April 21-23, 278–281.

Garcia-Holgado, A., Gonzalez-Gonzalez, C.S., and Jose-Garcia-Penalvo, F. (2021). Introduction of the Gender Perspective in the University Teaching: A Study About Inclusive Language in Spanish. 2021 IEEE Global Engineering Education Conference, EDUCON 2021, April 21-23, 1669–1673.

Garcia-Holgado, A., Verdugo-Castro, S., Dominguez, A., Hernandez-Armenta, I., Garcia-Penalvo, F.J., Vazquez-Ingelmo, A., and Sanchez-Gomez, M.C. (2021). The Experience of Women Students in Engineering and Mathematics Careers: A Focus Group Study. 2021 IEEE Global Engineering Education Conference, EDUCON 2021, April 21-23, 50–56.

Garcia-Ramos, L., Pena-Baena, R., Garcia-Holgado, A., Diaz, A.C., and Calle, M.G. (2021). Empowering Young Women in the Caribbean Region in STEM. 2021 IEEE Global Engineering Education Conference, EDUCON 2021, April 21-23, 1087–1092.

Goings, F., Wilson, N.L., Equiza, A., Lefsrud, L.M., and Willis, L.M. (2021). Margaret-Ann Armour and WISEST: An Incredible Legacy in Advancing Women in Science, Technology, Engineering, and Mathematics (STEM) and the Work Still to Do. *Canadian Journal of Chemistry* 99(8): 646–652.

Gok, T. (2021). The Development of the STEM (Science, Technology, Engineering, and Mathematics) Attitude and Motivation Survey Towards Secondary School Students. *International Journal of Cognitive Research in Science, Engineering and Education* (IJCRSEE) 9(1): 105–119.

Gomez, J., Tayebi, A., and Delgado, C. (2021). Factors That Influence Career Choice in Engineering Students in Spain: A Gender Perspective. *IEEE Transactions on Education* 65(1): 81–92.

Gonzalez, C., Garcia-Holgado, A., Plaza, P., Castro, M., Peixoto, A., Merino, J., Sancristobal, E., Menacho, A., Urbano, D., Blazquez, M., Garcia-Loro, F., Restivo, T., Strachan, R., Diaz, P., Plaza, I., Fernandez, C., Lord, S., Rover, D., Chan, R., ... Abreu, P. (2021). Gender and STEAM as Part of the MOOC STEAM4ALL. 2021 IEEE Global Engineering Education Conference, EDUCON 2021, April 21-23, 1630–1634.

Gonzalez-Gonzalez, C.S. and Garcia-Holgado, A. (2021). Strategies to Gender Mainstreaming in Engineering Studies: A Workshop with Teachers. 21st International Conference on Human-Computer Interaction, INTERACCION 2021, Sept. 22-24, Universidad de Malaga, Instituto de Salud Carlos III.

Gonzalez-Mendivil, J.A., Rodriguez-Paz, M.X., and Zamora-Hernandez, I. (2021). Women in Engineering Academic Programs: A Dynamic Modelling Approach for Southern Mexico. 2021 IEEE Global Engineering Education Conference, EDUCON 2021, April 21-23, 178–183.

Groher, I., Sabitzer, B., Demarle-Meusel, H., Kuka, L., and Hofer, A. (2021). Work-in-progress: Closing the Gaps: Diversity in Programming Education. 2021 IEEE Global Engineering Education Conference, EDUCON 2021, April 21-23, 1449–1453.

Hamlet, L.C., Roy, A., Scalone, G., Lee, R., Poleacovschi, C., and Kaminsky, J. (2021). Gender and Engineering Identity Among Upper-Division Undergraduate Students. *Journal of Management in Engineering* 37(2).

Happe, L. and Buhnova, B. (2021). Frustrations Steering Women away from Software Engineering. *IEEE Software* 1(7).

Harcey, S.R., Steidl, C.R., and Werum, R. (2021). STEM Degrees and Military Service: An Intersectional Analysis. *Armed Forces and Society* (0095327X), 1.

Hardin, C.D. (2021). Gender Differences in Hackathons as a Non-traditional Educational Experience. *ACM Transactions on Computing Education* 21(2): 1–30.

Heng, J. (2021). Championing Research. *TCE: The Chemical Engineer* 958: 42–43.

Hirshfield, L.J. and Chachra, D. (2021). Complex Systems: Interactions Between Gender and Project Context on Confidence of First-Year Engineering

Students. *International Journal of Engineering Education* 37(4): 1090–1107.

Hsu, H.-C. K. and Memon, N. (2021). Crossing the Bridge to STEM: Retaining Women Students in an Online CS Conversion Program. *ACM Transactions on Computing Education* 21(2): 1–16.

Hu, A., Wu, X., and Chen, T. (2021). Changing Subjective Wellbeing Across the College Life: Survey Evidence from China. *Chinese Sociological Review* 53(4): 409–429.

Huaman Sarmiento, L.K., Mego Sanchez, C., Iraola-Real, l., Huaman Sarmiento, M.L., and Mego Sanchez, H.D. (2021). "Women Are Less Anxious in Systems Engineering": A Comparative Study in Two Engineering Careers. 2nd International Conference on Advances in Emerging Trends and Technologies, ICAETT 2020, Oct. 26-30, 1302, 325–334.

Hwang, S. (2021). The Role of Psychological Well-Being in Women Undergraduate Students' Engineering Self-Efficacy and Major Satisfaction. *International Journal of Engineering Education* 37(4): 999–1012.

Infante-Perea, M., Navarro-Astor, E., and Roman-Onsalo, M. (2021). Sex, Age, Work Experience, and Relatives in Building Engineering Career Development. *Journal of Management in Engineering* 37(5).

Jackson, A., Mentzer, N., and Kramer-Bottiglio, R. (2021). Increasing Gender Diversity in Engineering Using Soft Robotics. *Journal of Engineering Education* 110(1): 143–160.

Jeffers, A.E. (2021). The COVID-19 Pandemic Is Widening the Gap for Women in STEM. *Computing in Science and Engineering* 23(3): 96–98.

Jensen, K.J. and Cross, K.J. (2021). Engineering Stress Culture: Relationships Among Mental Health, Engineering Identity, and Sense of Inclusion. *Journal of Engineering Education* 110(2): 371–392.

Jimenez, P.P., Pascual, J., Espinoza, J., Martin, S.S., and Guidi, F. (2021). Pedagogical Innovations with a Gender Approach to Increase Computer Programming Self-Efficacy in Engineering Students. 2021 IEEE Global Engineering Education Conference, EDUCON 2021, April 21-23, 322–328.

John, C. and Meinel, C. (2021). How Does the Corona Pandemic Influence Women's Participation in Massive Open Online Courses in STEM? 2021 IEEE Global Engineering Education Conference, EDUCON 2021, April 21-23, 448–455.

Jung, S.E. and Lee, K. (2021). A Girls Gendered Engagement in Designing and Building Robots. *International Journal of Technology and Design Education* 9(24).

Kashyap, R. and Verkroost, F.C.J. (2021). Analysing Global Professional Gender Gaps Using LinkedIn Advertising Data. *EPJ Data Science* 10(1).

Keku, D., Paige, F., Shealy, T., and Godwin, A. (2021). Recognizing Differences in Underrepresented Civil Engineering Students' Career Satisfaction Expectations and College Experiences. *Journal of Management in Engineering* 37(4).

Kelliher, R. (2021). Academic Pipeline Programs for Underrepresented Students That Work. *Diverse: Issues in Higher Education* 38(13): 6–6.

Kim, J.S. (2021). What Can Women's Networks Do to Close the Gender Gap in STEM? *Pure and Applied Chemistry* 93(8): 937–944.

King-Lewis, A., Shan, Y., and Ivey, M. (2021). Gender Bias and Its Impact on Self-Concept in Undergraduate and Graduate Construction Education Programs in the United States. *Journal of Construction Engineering and Management* 147(11).

Koerner, E.R. (2021). Inventor, Devoted Daughter, or Lover? Uncovering the Life and Work of Victorian Naval Engineer Henrietta Vansittart (1833-1883). *Science Museum Group Journal* 15: 29–52.

Kozan, K., Menekse, M., and Anwar, S. (2021). Exploring the Role of STEM Content, Professional Skills, and Support Service Needs in Predicting Engineering Students' Mid-College Academic Success. *International Journal of Engineering Education* 37(3): 690–700.

Lappe, A.K.R., Torales-Sanchez, D., Fuentes, A.B.G., and Caratozzolo, P. (2021). Work in Progress: Addressing Barriers for Women in STEM in Mexico. 2021 IEEE Global Engineering Education Conference, EDUCON 2021, April 21-23, 1600–1604.

Lara-Prieto, V., Garcia-Garcia, R.M., Ruiz-Cantisani, M.I., Burgos-Lopez, M.Y., Caratozzolo, P., Uribe-Lam, E., Romero-Robles, L.E., and Membrillo-Hernandez, J. (2021). Women Engineers Empowerment Through Linked Experiences. 2021 IEEE Global Engineering Education Conference, EDUCON 2021, April 21-23, 289–293.

Lecorchick, D., Bonda, J., Isabell, T., and Shapiro, D. (2021). Career Technology and Engineering Education Professionals: A Woman's Journey Through Reflections. 2021 IEEE Global Engineering Education Conference, EDUCON 2021, April 21-23, 2021, 1322–1328.

Li, N., Fan, W., Wiesner, M., Arbona, C., and Hein, S. (2021). Adapting the Utrecht-Management of Identity Commitments Scale to Assess Engineering Identity Formation. *Journal of Engineering Education* 110(4): 885–901.

Lima, D.A., Ferreira, M.E.A., and Silva, A.F.F. (2021). Machine Learning and Data Visualization to Evaluate a Robotics and Programming Project Targeted for Women. *Journal of Intelligent and Robotic Systems: Theory and Applications* 103(1).

Lin, Z., Chen, K., and Liu, Y. (2021). Mixed Methods Analysis: Investigating the Influences of Social Gender and Family Gender Perceptions on Female Students' Professional Choices and Planning in Their Last Year of College. 10th International Conference on Educational and Information Technology, ICEIT 2021, Jan. 18-20, 226–232.

Lonka, K., Ketonen, E., and Vermunt, J.D. (2021). University Students' Epistemic Profiles, Conceptions of Learning, and Academic Performance. *Higher Education* (00181560) 81(4): 775–793.

Lord, S.M., Ohland, M.W., Long, R.A., and Layton, R.A. (2021). Quantitative Exploration of International Female and Male Students in Undergraduate Engineering Programs in the USA. 2021 IEEE Global Engineering Education Conference, EDUCON 2021, April 21-23, 184–188.

Lymperaki-Besson, E., Kotsifakou, K.M., Kotsifakos, D., and Douligeris, C. (2021). Women and Digital Economy: Culture Change or Perpetuation of Inequalities? 2021 IEEE Global Engineering Education Conference, EDUCON 2021, April 21-23, 973–982.

MacDonald, F. and Durdyev, S. (2021). What Influences Women to Study Architectural, Engineering, or Construction (AEC) Majors? *Journal of Civil Engineering Education* 147(2).

Male, S., Marinelli, M., and Chapman, E. (2021). Creating Inclusive Engineering and Computer Science Classes — The Impact of COVID-19 on Student Experiences and Perceptions of Gender Inclusivity. 2021 IEEE Global Engineering Education Conference, EDUCON 2021, April 21-23, 456–458.

Marinelli, M., Male, S., and Lord, L. (2021). Women Engineers' Advancement to Management and Leadership Roles — Enabling Resources and Implications for Higher Education. 2021 IEEE Global Engineering Education Conference, EDUCON 2021, April 21-23, 463–467.

Maurer, J.A., Choi, D., and Hur, H. (2021). Building a Diverse Engineering and Construction Industry: Public and Private Sector Retention of Women in the Civil Engineering Workforce. *Journal of Management in Engineering* 37(4).

McCall, M. (2021). Getting the Story Straight: How Conflicting Narratives About Communication Impact Women in Engineering. *Technical Communication Quarterly* 30(1): 89–103.

McGee, E.O., Main, J.B., Miles, M.L., and Cox, M.F. (2021). An Intersectional Approach to Investigating Persistence Among Women of Color Tenure-Track Engineering Faculty. *Journal of Women and Minorities in Science and Engineering* 27(1): 57–84.

Meintjes, E.M. (2021). Tania Samantha Douglas (1969-2021): Biomedical Engineer, Academic and Leader. *South African Journal of Science* 117(5/6): 6–6.

Melak, A. and Singh, S. (2021). Factors Affecting Women's Choice of Learning Engineering and Technology Education in Ethiopia. *IEEE Access* 9, 83887–83900.

Melde, K.L. (2021). Charting a Pathway to Leadership [Women in Engineering]. *IEEE Antennas and Propagation Magazine* 63(2): 107–110.

Migliaccio, C. (2021). DEI: Diversity, Equity, and Inclusion Committee [Women in Engineering]. *IEEE Antennas and Propagation Magazine* 63(4): 138–141.

Minnotte, K.L. and Pedersen, D.E. (2021). Turnover Intentions in the STEM Fields: The Role of Departmental Factors. *Innovative Higher Education* 46(1): 77–93.

Moè, A., Hausmann, M., and Hirnstein, M. (2021). Gender Stereotypes and Incremental Beliefs in STEM and Non-STEM Students in Three Countries: Relationships with Performance in Cognitive Tasks. *Psychological Research* 85(2): 554–567.

Monteiro, F., Leite, C., and Rocha, C. (2021). The Engineering Social Role Conception Promoted in the Engineering Courses' Advertising: Looking from the Point of View of Women. 2021 IEEE

Global Engineering Education Conference, EDU-CON 2021, April 21-23, 1407–1415.

Mouronte-Lopez, M.L. and Ceres, J.S. (2021). Analyzing Enrollment in Information and Communication Technology Programs and Use of Social Networks Based on Gender. *International Journal of Engineering Education* 37(5): 1215–1230.

Mouronte-López, M.L., García, A., Bautista, S., and Cortés, C. (2021). Analyzing the Gender Influence on the Interest in Engineering and Technical Subjects. *International Journal of Technology and Design Education* 31(4): 723–739.

Mujawamariya, D., Fournier, J., Adatia, S., and Mavriplis, C. (2021). Designing to Engineer a Safer World: It Is Imperative to Promote Engineering and Its Positive Effects on Women and Society, but Also to Make Girls and Women Aware That They Too Possess the Skills to Drive Change. *Technology and Engineering Teacher* 81(2): 8–14.

Naukkarinen, J. and Bairoh, S. (2021). Gender Differences in Professional Identities and Development of Engineering Skills Among Early Career Engineers in Finland. *European Journal of Engineering Education* 47(1): 85–101.

Nelson, L.K. and Zippel, K. (2021). From Theory to Practice and Back: How the Concept of Implicit Bias Was Implemented in Academe, and What This Means for Gender Theories of Organizational Change. *Gender and Society* 35(3): 330–357.

No Life But This: A Novel of Emily Warren Roebling. (2021). *Kirkus Reviews* 89(9): 167–168.

Nolazco-Flores, J.A. and Swain-Oropeza, R. (2021). Engineering School Women Faculty Evaluation in Tec21 Competence Educational Model. 2021 IEEE Global Engineering Education Conference, EDUCON 2021, April 21-23, 851–856.

Onuma, F.J. and Berhane, B.T. (2021). The Role of Family in the Educational Careers of Black Engineering Alumni. *Journal of Women and Minorities in Science and Engineering* 27(5): 83–118.

Orgeira-Crespo, P., Míguez-Álvarez, C., Cuevas-Alonso, M., and Rivo-López, E. (2021). An Analysis of Unconscious Gender Bias in Academic Texts by Means of a Decision Algorithm. *PLOS ONE* 16(9): 1–20.

Osten, V. (2021). Gender Differences in Job Searches by New Engineering Graduates in Canada. *Journal of Engineering Education* 110(3): 750–764.

Ouhbi, S. and Awad, M.A.M. (2021). The Impact of Combining Storytelling with Lecture on Female Students in Software Engineering Education. 2021 IEEE Global Engineering Education Conference, EDUCON 2021, April 21-23, 443–447.

Park, J.J., Salazar, C., Parikh, R.M., Zheng, J., Liwanag, A.M., and Dunewood, L. (2021). Connections Matter: Accessing Information About Education and Careers in STEM. *Journal of Women and Minorities in Science and Engineering* 27(6): 85–113.

Patrick, A., Borrego, M., and Riegle-Crumb, C. (2021). Post-graduation Plans of Undergraduate BME Students: Gender, Self-efficacy, Value, and Identity Beliefs. *Annals of Biomedical Engineering* 49(5): 1275–1287.

Patrick, A., Riegle-Crumb, C., and Borrego, M. (2021). Examining the Gender Gap in Engineering Professional Identification. *Journal of Women and Minorities in Science and Engineering* 27(1): 31–55.

Pietri, E.S., Johnson, I.R., Majid, S., and Chu, C. (2021). Seeing What's Possible: Videos Are More Effective than Written Portrayals for Enhancing the Relatability of Scientists and Promoting Black Female Students' Interest in STEM. *Sex Roles* 84(1/2): 14–33.

Pitt, R.N., Brockman, A., and Zhu, L. (2021). Parental Pressure and Passion: Competing Motivations for Choosing STEM and Non-STEM Majors Among Women Who Double-Major in Both. *Journal of Women and Minorities in Science and Engineering* 27(1): 1–29.

Poleacovschi, C., Javernick-Will, A., Wang, S., and Tong, T. (2021). Gendered Knowledge Accessibility: Evaluating the Role of Gender in Knowledge Seeking Among Engineers in the US. *Journal of Management in Engineering* 37(1).

Polmear, M., Chau, A.D., and Simmons, D.R. (2021). Intersection of Diversity, Out-of-Class Engagement, and Engineer of 2020 Outcomes for Civil Engineering Students. *Journal of Management in Engineering* 37(4).

Poscic, P., Candrlic, S., and Jaksic, D. (2021). Academic Maturity and Gender Differences in Students' Expectations from an ICT Study Program: A Survey. 23rd International Conference on Interactive Collaborative Learning, ICL 2020, Sept. 23-25, 1329, 509–520.

Purkovic, D., Suman, D., and Jelaska, I. (2021). Age and Gender Differences Between Pupils' Preferences in Teaching General and Compulsory Technology Education in Croatia. *International Journal of Technology and Design Education* 31(5): 919–937.

Rainey, K.D. (2021). *Upper-Division Thermal Physics Assessment Development and the Impacts of Race and Gender on Stem Participation.* Dissertations Abstracts International, 82-11B. Ann Arbor: ProQuest Dissertations & Theses, 2021.

Riegle-Crumb, C. and Peng, M. (2021). Examining High School Students' Gendered Beliefs About Math: Predictors and Implications for Choice of STEM College Majors. *Sociology of Education* 94(3): 227–248.

Rincon, R. (2021). Reaching Gender Equity in STEM Professions. *Hydraulics and Pneumatics* 74(5), 12–13.

Robles, L.E.R., Martinez, M.G.O., Prieto, V.L., Catinsani, M.I.R., and Salgado, R.R. (2021). Strengthening of Women's Leadership in STEM Educational Environment Through Social Networks: Case of Success with International Network. 2021 IEEE Global Engineering Education Conference, EDUCON 2021, April 21-23, 1061-1065.

Ross, M.S., Huff, J.L., and Godwin, A. (2021). Resilient Engineering Identity Development Critical to Prolonged Engagement of Black Women in Engineering. *Journal of Engineering Education* 110(1): 92–113.

Ruiz-Cantisani, M.I., Lara-Prieto, V., Garcia-Garcia, R.M., Ortiz, M.G., Flores, E.G.R., and Romero-Robles, L.E. (2021). Mentoring Program: Women Supporting Women. 2021 IEEE Global Engineering Education Conference, EDUCON 2021, April 21-23, 552-556.

Ruiz-Cantisani, M.I., Lopez-Ruiz, D.I., Suarez-Cavazos, N., Novelo-Villegas, J., Rincon-Flores, E.G., and Burgos-Lopez, M.Y. (2021). STEM Gender Equity: Empowering Women in Vulnerable Environments. 2021 IEEE Global Engineering Education Conference, EDUCON 2021, April 21-23, 499-504.

Salas-Morera, L., Ruiz-Bustos, R., Cejas-Molina, M.A., Olivares-Olmedilla, J.L., Garcia-Hernandez, L., and Palomo-Romero, J.M. (2021). Understanding Why Women Don't Choose Engineering Degrees. *International Journal of Technology and Design Education* 31(2): 325–338.

Schmitt, M. (2021). Women Engineers on Their Way to Leadership: The Role of Social Support Within Engineering Work Cultures. *Engineering Studies* 13(1): 30–52.

Secules, S., Sochacka, N.W., Huff, J.L., and Walther, J. (2021). The Social Construction of Professional Shame for Undergraduate Engineering Students. *Journal of Engineering Education* 110(4): 861–884.

Silva Soares, A.K., da Silva Nascimento, B., Silvestre da Silva, J., da Cruz Serejo Barbosa, N., and Fernandes Kamazaki, D. (2021). Psychometric Properties of the Academic Major Satisfaction Scale (AMSS) in Brazilian College Students. *Propiedades Psicométricas de La Escala de Satisfacción Del Curso Académico (ESCA) En Estudiantes Universitarios Brasileños* 39(1): 229–251.

Simmons, D.R. and Chau, A.D. (2021). Factors Predicting Out-of-Class Participation for Underrepresented Groups in STEM. *Journal of STEM Education: Innovations and Research* 22(1): 52–61.

Sya'bandari, Y., Aini, R.Q., Rusmana, A.N., and Ha, M. (2021). Indonesian Students' STEM Career Motivation: A Study Focused on Gender and Academic Level. 2020 International Joint Conference on STEM Education, IJCSE 2020, Nov. 18-19, 1957(1).

Szakonyi, A., Dawson, M., Chellasamy, H., and Vassilakos, A. (2021). Non-Traditional Education to Advance Women in Computing Careers in the St. Louis Metro Region. 2021 IEEE Global Engineering Education Conference, EDUCON 2021, April 21-23, 1093-1097.

Tan, L., Main, J.B., and Darolia, R. (2021). Using Random Forest Analysis to Identify Student Demographic and High School-Level Factors That Predict College Engineering Major Choice. *Journal of Engineering Education* 110(3): 572–593.

Tapia, L. (2021). Retrospective on a Watershed Moment for IEEE Robotics and Automation Society Gender Diversity [Women in Engineering]. *IEEE Robotics & Automation Magazine* 28(3): 163–167.

Thébaud, S. and Taylor, C.J. (2021). The Specter of Motherhood: Culture and the Production of Gendered Career Aspirations in Science and Engineering. *Gender and Society* 35(3): 395–421.

Thomas, S. (2021). Best Practices in Robotics Education: Perspectives from an IEEE RAS Women in Engineering Panel [Women in Engineering]. *IEEE Robotics and Automation Magazine* 28(1): 12–15.

Thompson, D. (2021). Youth Empowerment Program Helps Female Engineers Succeed. *TD: Talent Development* 75(9): 14–15.

Thurner, V., Bottcher, A., and Hafner, T. (2021). A Detailed Analysis of Gender Differences in the Course of CS-Studies. 2021 IEEE Global Engineering Education Conference, EDUCON 2021, April 21-23, 482–491.

Tomko, M., Aleman, M.W., Newstetter, W., Nagel, R.L., and Linsey, J. (2021). Participation Pathways for Women into University Makerspaces. *Journal of Engineering Education* 110(3): 700–717.

Tranquada, S., Correia, N., and Baras, K. (2021). Using Technology to Visualize Gender Bias. 18th IFIP TC 13 International Conference on Human-Computer Interaction, INTERACT 2021, Aug. 30-Sept. 3, 12936 LNCS, 186–194.

True-Funk, A., Poleacovschi, C., Jones-Johnson, G., Feinstein, S., Smith, K., and Luster-Teasley, S. (2021). Intersectional Engineers: Diversity of Gender and Race Microaggressions and Their Effects in Engineering Education. *Journal of Management in Engineering* 37(3).

Urbano, D., Menezes, P., de Fatima Chouzal, M., and Restivo, M.T. (2021). A Case Study of AR Technology and Engineering Students: Is There a Gender Gap? 17th International Conference on Remote Engineering and Virtual Instrumentation, REV 2020, Feb. 26-28, 1231 AISC, 330–337.

Veldman, J., Van Laar, C., Thoman, D.B., and Van Soom, C. (2021). "Where Will I Belong More?": The Role of Belonging Comparisons Between STEM Fields in High School Girls' STEM Interest. *Social Psychology of Education* 24(5): 1363–1387.

Vieira, C.C. and Vasconcelos, M. (2021). Using Facebook Ads Data to Assess Gender Balance in STEM: Evidence from Brazil. 30th World Wide Web Conference, WWW 2021, April 19-23, 145–153.

Vujovic, M., Amarasinghe, I., Hernández-Leo, D., and Gamage, K. (2021). Studying Collaboration Dynamics in Physical Learning Spaces: Considering the Temporal Perspective Through Epistemic Network Analysis. *Sensors* (14248220) 21(9): 2898–2898.

Welty, K. (2021). Literature-Based STEM: Leveraging Children's Books to Teach Science, Technology, Engineering and Mathematics. *Elementary STEM Journal* 25(4): 33–36.

Werz, J.M., Schmitt, M., Borowski, E., Wilkesmann, U., and Isenhardt, I. (2021). An Online-Tool for Career Planning of Women in STEM: From Research to Application. 2021 IEEE Global Engineering Education Conference, EDUCON 2021, April 21-23, 1019–1025.

Whitcomb, K.M., Maries, A., and Singh, C. (2021). Examining Gender Differences in a Mechanical Engineering and Materials Science Curriculum. *International Journal of Engineering Education* 37(5): 1261–1273.

Wiggins, M.D. and Boggs, G.R. (2021). Toward Gender Equality in Technology Careers. *Diverse: Issues in Higher Education* 38(8): 36–36.

Williams, K. (2021). Preparing Engineers to Do Good in the World: Barabino Creating Supportive Environments. *IEEE Women in Engineering Magazine* 15(1): 16–20.

Wilson, N.L., Dance, T., Pei, W., Sanders, R.S., and Ulrich, A.C. (2021). Learning, Experiences, and Actions Towards Advancing Gender Equity in Engineering as Aspiring Men's Allyship Group. *Canadian Journal of Chemical Engineering* 99(10): 2124–2137.

Woerpel, H. (2021). On the Lookout for the Industry's Leading Ladies. *Engineered Systems* 38(8): 11–11.

Yang, J.A., Sherard, M.K., Julien, C., and Borrego, M. (2021). Resistance and Community-Building in LGBTQ+ Engineering Students. *Journal of Women and Minorities in Science and Engineering* 27(4).

Zhao, D., Muntean, C.H., Chis, A.E., and Muntean, G.-M. (2021). Learner Attitude, Educational Background, and Gender Influence on Knowledge Gain in a Serious Games-Enhanced Programming Course. *IEEE Transactions on Education* 64(3): 308–316.

*"SWE provides opportunities for me to engage in project management and leadership roles that build my confidence as an engineer."*

**Join or renew today at** membership.swe.org

# Profiles and Perspectives from Behind the Research

Complementing this issue's analysis of the past 20 years of literature reviews, *SWE Magazine* spoke with some of the researchers whose work has been cited over the years.

By Sandra Guy, SWE Contributor

What does social science research tell us about the persistent underrepresentation of women in engineering? How much is understood about women's experiences in engineering education, to obtaining undergraduate and graduate degrees, and in the workplace?

In an effort to find out, in 2001 *SWE Magazine* started its annual review of the research literature on women in engineering, and more broadly, the STEM professions. For the past 20 years, the literature review authors have examined peer-reviewed articles in academic journals from a variety of social science disciplines, publishing an analysis of each year's most interesting or insightful work, and providing an extensive bibliography that averaged more than 200 individual works.

With two decades of reviews behind us, this year *SWE Magazine* is providing a retrospective analysis of those reviews. In keeping with this examination, below are profiles of some of the researchers whose works have been cited over the years. It's worth noting that trends and interests change over time, as do areas of consensus and differences among researchers and research findings.

## DIANA BILIMORIA, PH.D.

"WE NEED A CULTURAL MINDSET SHIFT TO BECOME MORE INCLUSIVE. WE NEED TO RECOGNIZE WHAT THAT TAKES, HOW WE GET THERE, AND WHAT DOES THAT LOOK LIKE IN A GRANULAR WAY — AND PUT POLICIES IN PLACE SO THE RIGHT INFORMATION IS THERE WHEN DECISIONS LIKE HIRING AND PROMOTIONS ARE MADE."

– Diana Bilimoria, Ph.D., KeyBank professor and chair of organizational behavior, Case Western Reserve University

**Diana Bilimoria, Ph.D.**, has, in her words, enabled, equipped, empowered, and encouraged people, teams, organizations, and institutions to become aware of and remedy patterns of inequities that constrain women's opportunities.

"Decision-makers can make choices informed by a diversity perspective to include people from different genders, ethnicities, cultures, and other aspects," said Dr. Bilimoria, the KeyBank professor and chair of organizational behavior at the Weatherhead School of Management at Case Western Reserve University in Cleveland.

She's been at it for three decades.

Her efforts have resulted in measurable results, about which she has published extensively.

She said her aim has always been to provide tools so that people "see how they can become more inclusive in bringing in diverse talent and employing that talent to drive their organization forward."

Dr. Bilimoria started by examining women's roles on corporate boards of directors as part of her Ph.D. dissertation and found that company boards' most powerful committees — executive, audit, and compensation committees, for example — were exclusively male. Women were relegated to less-powerful committees such as public relations and community affairs.

"Even at this highest level, where board members are extremely well qualified, well educated, and well experienced, women faced subtle discrimination," said Dr. Bilimoria, whose work was published in top academic journals as she embarked on her career.

Now, the average number of female corporate directors stands at 3.4 out of an average board size of 11.1, according to a Bloomberg analysis of the S&P 500 companies. The increase for Black women in 2021 was twice the rate for women overall, but Black women hold only 4% of S&P 500 board seats, the data show.

Dr. Bilimoria supports efforts to set goals for equity, diversity, inclusion, and leadership. "Goal setting is very important at every level — individual, team, and collective," she said.

She next tackled academia by helping write a National Science Foundation ADVANCE institutional transformation grant, aimed at increasing women's representation and advancement in academic science and engineering careers at Case Western.

Her work, starting in 2003, along with colleagues, made them pioneers in bringing into academia initiatives such as executive coaching, mentoring, and systemic leadership development for women faculty and institutional leaders.

"Our experiment was to bring effective practices in business and industry into the academic world," Dr. Bilimoria said.

Her work led to other grants and eventually a book, *Gender Equity in Science and Engineering: Advancing Change in Higher Education* (2015), co-authored with Xiangfen Liang, Ph.D.

The research revealed that women's issues aren't monolithic because certain groups — such as women of color and people who identify as LGBTQA+ — experienced greater marginalization.

Together with Lynn T. Singer, Ph.D., Distinguished University Professor at Case Western Reserve University, Dr. Bilimoria led two subsequent NSF ADVANCE projects: the 2009–2012 IDEAL program that brought together six research universities to address issues of gender, diversity, inclusion, and equity, and the 2015–2019 IDEAL-N program that included 10 research universities.

Dr. Bilimoria also served as the research director of a multi-university NSF Alliances for

## Inspired to Study Human Behavior

Diana Bilimoria, Ph.D., followed her father and her brother into the world of accounting and finance, but it was her later experience in the hotel industry that led her to study human behavior.

She earned her undergraduate degree in accounting and finance where she grew up — in Mumbai, India — and obtained the equivalent of an MBA focused on human resource management.

That's when she started working in human resources, training, development, planning, and strategy.

"I found HR to be more interesting," said Dr. Bilimoria, who came to the United States to earn her Ph.D. in business administration from the University of Michigan. "I still love doing my own accounting. But [HR] was a more appealing and attractive area. You had to work with people [to] solve real issues and real problems. There were consequences to everything."

Graduate Education and the Professoriate project to advance underrepresented doctoral students to the STEM professoriate.

And her research, along with Abigail J. Stewart, Ph.D., in "'Don't Ask, Don't Tell': The Academic Climate for Lesbian, Gay, Bisexual, and Transgender Faculty in Science and Engineering" (2009) revealed that LGBT faculty members experienced LGBT identity-based invisibility, rejection, pressure, and isolation in many science and engineering departments. Dr. Stewart is the Sandra Schwartz Tangri Distinguished University Professor of Psychology and Women's and Gender Studies at the University of Michigan.

"A more inclusive work environment — one in which LGBT faculty felt accepted as whole persons — would not only be more humane, but might also facilitate enhanced scientific productivity from these faculty and their colleagues," the research concluded.

"The goal is to create workplaces that are more inclusive, energizing, motivating, and supportive," Dr. Bilimoria said. "We want to see academic institutions doing the kind of research and education work, dissemination, and outreach that meet the needs of the world today."

"It is the right response for the moment," she said. "We need a cultural mindset shift to become more inclusive. We need to recognize what that takes, how we get there, and what does that look like in a granular way — and put policies in place so the right information is there when decisions like hiring and promotions are made."

Dr. Bilimoria said she is hopeful for the future. "It is about incremental change," she said. "Higher education institutions are steeped in history and legacy. That's their strength."

"Yet there are periods for transformative institutional change. There's a role for both. Incremental moves the needle within the system until the time is right for something more transformative."

## ERIN A. CECH, PH.D.

"THROUGH COPING STRATEGIES WHICH CAN REQUIRE IMMENSE AMOUNTS OF ADDITIONAL EMOTIONAL AND ACADEMIC EFFORT, SEXUAL MINORITY STUDENTS NAVIGATE A CHILLY AND HETERONORMATIVE ENGINEERING CLIMATE BY 'PASSING' AS HETEROSEXUAL, 'COVERING' OR DOWNPLAYING CULTURAL CHARACTERISTICS ASSOCIATED WITH LGB IDENTITIES, AND GARNERING EXPERTISE TO MAKE THEMSELVES INDISPENSABLE TO OTHERS."

– From "Navigating the Heteronormativity of Engineering: The Experiences of Lesbian, Gay, and Bisexual Students," Erin Cech, Ph.D., and Tom Waidzunas, Ph.D.

Erin A. Cech, Ph.D.'s body of work verifies a troubling picture of engineering as a heteronormative, male-dominated profession where a majority feels threatened by people who fail to conform to a heterosexual worldview, and who also distrust women's and mothers' ability to focus on their work.

But Dr. Cech, an associate professor of sociology at the University of Michigan, also sees glimmers of hope in a world where the #MeToo and Black Lives Matter movements have galvanized women and racially minoritized communities; the COVID pandemic has empowered workers, and even the titans of Wall Street are requiring publicly traded companies to show progress in their diversity and inclusion goals.

Her evidence, collected throughout the past decade, shows how far engineering education and the profession remain from a perfectly functioning meritocracy.

In 2011, Dr. Cech released an article in *Engineering Studies*, with Tom Waidzunas, Ph.D., that revealed lesbian, gay, and bisexual students enrolled in engineering described a "heteronormative culture that forced the students to 'pass' as heterosexual or to downplay characteristics associated with their LGB identities."

Because colleges and universities don't ask students their sexual identities, the researchers collected data by interviewing students and holding

## A Grandmother's Struggles Heightened Her Awareness of Difference

Groundbreaking research — into the need to divorce one's passion from one's work, and on the engineering culture's corrosive effects on mothers and on LGBTQA+ persons — all started with Erin A. Cech's grandmother.

An associate professor of sociology at the University of Michigan, Erin Cech, Ph.D., grew up in Bozeman, Montana, where she says she was struck by how different it was for her maternal grandmother, Alice Walsh, who was blind, to move through the world.

Dr. Cech, with her dad, who worked as an electrical engineer, and her mom, a special education teacher, visited her grandmother frequently in a town 90 miles from their home. "I'd lead (my grandmother) onto buses as a kid," Dr. Cech recalled. "I learned how to tell her when to step up on curbs and [to go] down stairs."

"She lived by herself and managed the challenges of a 100-year-old house," Dr. Cech said. "She had an incredible network of friends, and to watch her navigate her life was amazing and inspirational.

"But it was also quite frustrating. She couldn't read newspapers. She'd get boxes of cassette tapes sent once every few months [of newspapers read aloud]. But it was news from five months before."

Dr. Cech also became aware that her grandmother, who operated mechanical calculators called comptometers at the local electric company before she lost her sight, trained male engineers to do the calculations but had no opportunities to advance on her own.

And Dr. Cech, who identifies as queer, experienced a masculine and heteronormative environment in her college engineering classes.

As one of only two or three women in her electrical engineering classes, Dr. Cech said she didn't dare speak up against the homophobic jokes or the sexist mnemonic devices that students used to remember color coding on electronic resistors in her electronics labs.

These personal experiences, and hearing about marginalization experiences among her classmates of color, propelled Dr. Cech to investigate processes of social inequality within STEM.

She said she realized that, if she wanted to help bring about social change, she needed more training in theoretical and methodological ways to understand these inequalities. So she added a sociology major as an undergraduate and pursued a Ph.D. in sociology.

Dr. Cech said a "ray of hope" has emerged in the grassroots Out in Science, Technology, Engineering and Mathematics (oSTEM), with more than 130 student chapters as well as an unspecified number of professional chapters, according to the nonprofit's website. oSTEM welcomes allies and lists seven affinity groups: Ace/Aro, (Dis)Ability, Womxn, InQUEERy, Middle Sexualities, Race and Ethnicity, and Trans and Non-Binary.

"There's a lot of movement in the student space and more engagement today than even a few years ago," Dr. Cech said. "It's important that students and academics can have that kind of space to talk with others, to mentor, and to be mentored."

focus groups. They posted flyers around the engineering buildings and wrote notes on chalkboards of engineering lecture halls advertising the study.

"Just the very act of writing, 'Are you a gay, lesbian, or bisexual engineering student?' on the board in an engineering classroom felt subversive at the time," Dr. Cech said.

Drs. Cech and Waidzunas conducted in-depth qualitative interviews with LBG-identifying engineering students — many of whom were not open about their sexuality to anyone else in the college.

They found that, "through coping strategies which can require immense amounts of additional emotional and academic effort, sexual minority students navigate a chilly and heteronormative engineering climate by 'passing' as heterosexual, 'covering' or downplaying cultural characteristics associated with LGB identities, and garnering expertise to make themselves indispensable to others."

"These additional work burdens are often accompanied by academic and social isolation, making engineering school a hostile place for many LGB-identifying students," the study concluded. "This research provides an opportunity to theorize categories of inequality within engineering that do not have visible markers, and to consider them within a broader framework of intersectionality."

In 2016, Dr. Cech, Dr. Waidzunas, and Stephanie Farrell, Ph.D., professor in chemical engineering, surveyed 47 engineering deans and program directors and found that participants said they were somewhat or very supportive of many LGBTQA+ inclusion measures, but they were not necessarily willing to commit college resources to those measures.

Why? They were afraid of faculty pushback.

Dr. Cech's article with William Rothwell, a Ph.D. in sociology, published in the December 2018 issue of *Journal of Engineering Education*, found similar patterns among LGBTQ-identifying engineering students.

The students were more likely to feel marginalized, have their work devalued, and they suffer more negative health and wellness outcomes than their non-LGBTQ peers as a result.

In the engineering profession, Dr. Cech's work found similar results. Drs. Cech and Waidzunas' Jan. 15, 2021, article in *Science Advances* found that LGBTQ STEM professionals were more likely to experience career limitations, harassment, and professional devaluation than their non-LGBTQ peers. They were also more likely to intend to leave STEM.

A key takeaway is that engineering — both in academia and in the corporate world — needs to take seriously concerns about the inequities within their ranks, for the good of those marginalized and for the good of engineering in general, Dr. Cech said.

There's no time to lose.

The 2021 *Science Advances* article, based on representative survey data from more than 25,000 members of 21 STEM professional societies, revealed that LGBTQ professionals had a 50% higher likelihood of intending to leave their jobs — 22% versus 15% for non-LGBTQ STEM professionals. Also, 12% of LGBTQ professionals, compared with 8% of their non-LGBTQ peers, said they planned to leave their STEM professions in the next five years. Dr. Cech said she was heartened by news coverage of the findings in the magazines *Nature* and *Science*.

She said it's also a step forward that some professional societies welcome those who identify as LGBTQA+ and host training workshops, learning communities, and other resources to support their LGBTQA+ members.

Those circumstances are buoyed by the U.S. Supreme Court decision on June 15, 2020, that the 1964 Civil Rights Act protects gay, lesbian, and transgender employees from discrimination based on sexual orientation and gender identity.

Dr. Cech said she believes "there will be marginally more" tolerance among younger generations. "But I expect that to take quite a bit of time," she said.

## STEM PROVES BRUTAL FOR NEW PARENTS, PARTICULARLY FOR NEW MOMS

Dr. Cech has also researched how new parents get through the transition of taking care of new children while maintaining a hectic workload.

She and Mary Blair-Loy, Ph.D., (2019) found that men and women often leave full-time STEM employment after the birth of their first child, but that women are much more likely to do so by a 43% to 23% margin.

Even mothers who remain in the professional workforce full time encounter stereotypes painting them as less competent than equally qualified men and childless women, and face salary penalties and career barriers even while contributing the same dedicated work.

That's on top of Dr. Cech's gender studies research in 2013 that unveiled a $13,000 average wage gap between men and women in engineering. In that research, she found patterns of segregation, with women less likely to have access to the most culturally valued and well-paid job activities than equally qualified men engineers.

## NADYA A. FOUAD, PH.D., AND ROMILA SINGH, PH.D.

TROYE FOX, UNIVERSITY OF WISCONSIN–MILWAUKEE

"THE 'WORK TRUMPS EVERYTHING' KIND OF CULTURE HAS BEEN FORCED TO PIVOT TO A DIFFERENT MENTALITY. IT'S NOT WORK OR FAMILY, OR FAMILY OR WORK. LIFE IS BOTH."

– Nadya A. Fouad, Ph.D., distinguished professor, department of educational psychology, University of Wisconsin–Milwaukee

"WHAT GIVES ME RENEWED STRENGTH IS THAT WE'RE MUCH MORE OPEN AS LEADERS, EMPLOYEES, AND EDUCATORS TO TALK ABOUT THESE ISSUES. THESE ARE DIFFICULT CONVERSATIONS TO HAVE. IT'S SENSITIVE. IT HITS SOME RAW NERVES, BUT THEY ARE VERY NECESSARY TO HAVE BY CREATING OR REINFORCING SAFE SPACES AND SYSTEMS."

– Romila Singh, Ph.D., associate professor, organizations and strategic management, University of Wisconsin–Milwaukee

It's been a decade since **Nadya A. Fouad, Ph.D.,** and **Romila Singh, Ph.D.,** released their seminal work, "Stemming the Tide: Why Women Leave Engineering" (2011), based on 5,500 women answering a survey by pouring out their personal stories of being ignored, slighted, and mistreated in the engineering workplace.

The results shut down what Dr. Fouad, distinguished professor in the department of educational psychology (School of Education) at the University of Wisconsin–Milwaukee, called "the mantra from White male engineers that women want to have babies" and that's why they leave the profession.

"It's just infuriating enough to drive us crazy," she said. "[Women] leave because it's so toxic. It's not an excuse to go have a family and do something else."

Dr. Singh, associate professor, organizations and strategic management in the University of Wisconsin–Milwaukee Lubar School of Business, added, "There was no flexibility, and it was a huge trigger. They tried to make it work with inflexible policies and, after trying their best, decided, 'My salary doesn't justify my getting all kinds of qualified help [to raise my own children and to run the household].'"

The study also revealed that, though an organization's systems, policies, and actions matter, the way workers and managers interact — whether they support or undermine their women colleagues — had a profound influence on women engineers' satisfaction, commitment, and ultimately, their desire to leave their employer and/or the profession.

The same was true for men as well, based on the researchers' recent findings comparing men and women engineers' experiences with undermining behaviors at work. Their results revealed that a hostile, undermining work environment hurt retention and engagement of both male and female engineers.

Dr. Fouad is quick to note that the bottom line isn't just "women are good — men are bad."

"It's a systemic problem," she said. "Good workplaces work for everybody. Toxic workplaces hurt everybody."

It's about fixing the weak or broken systems, rather than trying to "fix women" to try to prevent their departure from companies and the engineering profession.

In fact, their research had found, pre-COVID, that the engineering profession pushed out men who felt that the workplace culture left little to no time for their families and compelled them to consider leaving their companies and the profession.

Drs. Singh and Fouad have now turned to the question unique to the gravest pandemic in American history: Will the COVID-19 pandemic turn the tide toward greater recognition and retention of women engineers?

They're going a step beyond their pre-COVID research — to find out the best ways teams become open to a variety of perspectives — and are now hitting at the heart of companies' and organizations' work policies that encourage or stifle creativity and innovation.

"Women have had to figure out how to teach and help with homework [for children] at home, or who's home when, with what kid, and who has the flexibility to figure out what to do on Tuesday," Dr. Fouad said.

The stress has only amplified for working parents, especially mothers, in making these daily juggling decisions during the pandemic.

Have corporate and academic leaders paid attention? Will they make policies that encourage men and women to take parental leave, give women an uplifting space where they can be promoted and treated fairly, and let women and men have the flexibility they need to have personal lives?

Or is it just back to the office, same old, same old? They're hopeful but realistic.

"Our models of what it takes to be seen as successful in the workplace — there's no going back [post-COVID] to the way it was earlier," Dr. Fouad said. "This has provided a test. If you're going to gauge me by whether I have kids [yelling] in the background (for both men and women) during a video call, or because I signed into my work at 10 a.m. and stayed past midnight, that's now a problem. The 'work trumps everything' kind of culture has been forced to pivot to a different mentality. It's not work or family, or family or work. Life is both."

Dr. Singh said she and Dr. Fouad have not only tirelessly shared their evidence-based research with leaders, but have also asked them how they're making systemic changes.

"Women are not looking for token roles," Dr. Singh said, "so you can say, 'We have a woman in the C-suite.' But that doesn't answer the deeper questions like, 'What are the systems and criteria in place for promotion to the C-suite roles, and are they being equitably applied?'"

In fact, Drs. Fouad and Singh's research has provided clear ways to keep women from fleeing the engineering profession. For example, women expressed dissatisfaction with a lack of security, good compensation, good working conditions, opportunities for advancement, and a sense of accomplishment at work.

COVID exposed enormous new cracks in the workplace security blanket. For example, C-suite turnover — among CEOs, chief financial officers, chief marketing officers, and chief technology officers — is at a record high.

"These situations are complex, involve multilayered issues, and touch many systems that trigger pulling back in some way," Dr. Singh said. "It's not easy to say, 'I'm burnt out. I need to put my own well-being above corporate goals.'"

# Instilled with Confidence and a "Can-do" Attitude, They Became Gender Equity Researchers

Never underestimate the power of a brilliant mother who believes in you and your success.

Just take for example the mothers of gender-equity-in-engineering researchers Nadya A. Fouad, Ph.D., and Romila Singh, Ph.D., authors of "Stemming the Tide: Why Women Leave Engineering," and tireless advocates of keeping and promoting women in engineering.

Dr. Fouad's mother, Maria Elisabeth Fouad, who passed away in 2009, was a cook and a linguist who felt the sting of unfairness when she was unable to leverage her expertise in the workplace after she came to America from her native Brazil. She started teaching Spanish at Iowa State University, where she and Dr. Fouad's father met while earning their graduate degrees, but she was limited without a Ph.D.

Yet she was "an absolute instiller of confidence," Dr. Fouad said. "She was a great champion. I have a younger brother. She believed that her kids could absolutely do no wrong."

Dr. Fouad's father, A.A. Fouad, was a prominent engineering professor at Iowa State University in Ames, Iowa. A member of the National Academy of Engineering who passed away in 2017, he supported Dr. Fouad throughout her career, helping her connect with engineering schools and students to help her collect valuable data and information.

Dr. Singh vividly remembers poring over her mother's draft drawings when she was growing up in the family's home in Bhilai, a steel manufacturing town in the eastern-central part of the state of Chhattisgarh in India. Her mom, a mechanical engineer who earned her degree in the 1950s, would bring home the blueprints from projects she was working on with MECON Limited. The consulting company provided services for design, engineering, consultancy, inspection, construction, and project management, among others.

"I thought it was the coolest thing ever — to see the drawings and to see her do electrical, plumbing, and other projects around the house," Dr. Singh said. "There was nothing she couldn't do. She'd rip up walls and redesign things around the house. She was all about having a 'can-do' approach and not taking no for an answer when faced with obstacles."

Dr. Singh's father, a mechanical engineer, worked second shift so that he and Dr. Singh's mother could both work.

"They took turns being at home," Dr. Singh said. "It never crossed my dad's mind that she would stay home full time and not work at all."

"This way of growing up established and imprinted on me that women engineers are as tough, as good, as capable, and as accomplished as male engineers. This was before I started primary school," Dr. Singh said. "The can-do attitude has been a persistent theme — that we can impact change and solve problems."

Dr. Singh earned her master's degree in psychology from the University of Delhi in India and her Ph.D. in organizational sciences from Drexel University in Philadelphia as a way to leverage her background to "get a deep dive into important issues of work/life balance and the attraction and retention of highly skilled professionals."

"The 'can-do' attitude was a bit of a dive when I started on a different path (studying for a doctorate) in a different country, and it took some time to regain my voice, and to start using my voice to advocate for myself and others."

Increasingly, athletes adored by millions of fans, from Simone Biles to Naomi Osaka to Michael Phelps and Gabriel Medina, are speaking out, she said. "At the peak of their amazing talents and careers, they're saying, 'I need to also take care of my mental health, my well-being.'"

That portends potential good news, Dr. Singh said.

"What gives me renewed strength is that we're much more open as leaders, employees, and educators to talk about these issues," she said. "These are difficult conversations to have. It's sensitive. It hits some raw nerves, but they are very necessary to have by creating or reinforcing safe spaces and systems."

"What still gives me optimism, despite some of the [inevitable public] derision faced by these athletes who opened up about prioritizing their well-being, is that it gives other people the courage to say, 'If they can be open about this, I can, too. It allows me to have the courage to speak about my own struggles, even if there is a huge price to pay for this.'"

The unspoken payoff for so many people is self-care and focusing on one's own well-being, Dr. Singh said.

## SUSAN M. LORD, PH.D.

"IT'S MORE ABOUT CHANGING ENGINEERING THAN ABOUT CHANGING WOMEN OR PEOPLE OF COLOR. WHAT WE NEED TO FIX IS OUR OWN CULTURE, TO BE MORE WELCOMING AND TO ALLOW FOR DIVERSITY INSTEAD OF PUNISHING OR PENALIZING."

– Susan Lord, Ph.D., chair and professor, department of integrated engineering, University of San Diego

Engineering students in **Susan M. Lord**'s circuits class — an oft-dreaded class toward their degrees — must find out where a key capacitor ingredient is mined. When they discover that it's a conflict mineral, they have to explain how they'd minimize its use.

The point? A prime ingredient in tantalum capacitors is considered the "blood diamond" of electronics. Tantalum is often mined amid armed conflict and human rights abuses as warring groups fight over mines and smuggling routes. Tantalum is sourced in countries such as the Democratic Republic of the Congo, Rwanda, Nigeria, and Brazil.

Next, the students are instructed to research a company's conflict mineral strategy. They answer questions such as, "How do you interpret the data? Look critically at the source of the data and how it is presented. Apple cites its own data. Is it reliable?"

If you remember circuits class as a dry, excruciating exercise, welcome to the new world of "integrated engineering." It's the result of decades of research and cooperative work with sociologists, cultural anthropologists, and like-minded educators.

In fact, Susan Lord, Ph.D., was a key player in creating the department of integrated engineering at the University of San Diego, which she chairs.

The university's Shiley-Marcos School of Engineering website proclaims, "Here, students tinker, collaborate, build, test and create innovative solutions that make a world of difference."

Students are graduated from the program with a degree in engineering. The goal is to nudge the students, throughout their studies, to ask themselves, "What am I called to do? How do I want to use my talents in the world?" Dr. Lord said.

Another aim is to let students envision a future

in which their work isn't split from their dreams, hobbies, and authentic selves. Perhaps a first-year engineer has little influence on the job, but she could volunteer for pro bono work that would make a huge difference in the community, Dr. Lord said.

"I talk about my children," said Dr. Lord, the mother of two college-age daughters. "It's just as important for boys, too, to say, 'I love what I do. But I don't do it 24/7 and that's OK.'"

She can now laugh about being admonished early in her career by a male professor who said that she couldn't possibly be an electrical engineering professor if she didn't have an oscilloscope in her garage. Isn't that what she did in her spare time?

## Following Her Father's Footsteps, She Experienced the Gender Gap

Her deep experience in engineering education leadership provided a unique platform for Susan M. Lord, Ph.D., to influence engineering teaching reforms.

She serves as co-director of the National Effective Teaching Institute. As a fellow of the IEEE and the American Society for Engineering Education, she served as general co-chair of the Frontiers in Education Conference, president of the IEEE Education Society, and associate editor of the *IEEE Transactions on Education* and the *Journal of Engineering Education*.

Dr. Lord first experienced engineering education's culture when she followed in her dad's footsteps (he was a metallurgical engineer who taught at Drexel University in Philadelphia) in her own way by earning a dual undergraduate degree in electrical engineering and materials science from Cornell University and her master's and Ph.D. in electrical engineering from Stanford University.

"I thought that my experience would be like [my dad's]," she said. "But I found out that being a female was a big deal. I felt that sense of not belonging. I was the only female of 25 in my research group. My male peers would ask me, 'What do women think?'"

"I had no idea how to answer that, but I thought, 'Let me find out,'" Dr. Lord recalled. "I went to feminist studies classes. I learned about gaps. It gave me a language to interpret what I was experiencing in my life."

"I don't want my students or my colleagues to feel the way that I did," she said.

As her mother and paternal grandparents before her, Dr. Lord turned to teaching, to try to accomplish those goals. Her instincts in leading the mission no doubt stemmed from her Italian immigrant maternal grandparents, who worked in retail and ran a bread delivery business.

She said she's a realist in that culture is slow to change, especially a system such as engineering that has been designed to support uniformity rather than diversity. In a typical engineering classroom in America, she noted, you'd expect to find two-thirds of the students to be white men and fewer than one in five to be women.

But Dr. Lord is hopeful when she sees her own classrooms in integrated engineering, which this year comprise 36% to 78% women — far above the national average. While most engineering classrooms are 77% white, her classes have been about 50% white. She said she believes this shows that the integrated engineering approach is attracting a broader range of people.

As she had hoped, the students experience a more welcoming culture than she did and learn to think about and practice engineering in more holistic ways.

"They are poised to make a difference in addressing the greatest challenges of our world," Dr. Lord said, "today and in the future."

Well, she's never had an oscilloscope in her garage and now she's a Fellow of the IEEE and a tenured professor.

"There have to be multiple ways of success," Dr. Lord said.

## A PASSION BORN OF PERSONAL EXPERIENCE AND BREAKTHROUGH RESEARCH

Dr. Lord's zeal to encourage engineering students to critically analyze data, realize subtle interconnections, and see the field in new ways — and be better prepared for the workplace as a result — stems from her own college experience and her research with Michelle Camacho, Ph.D., a sociologist and cultural anthropologist, in unearthing Latinas' battles with exclusionary forces that shape the culture of engineering.

"Real engineering is messy," Dr. Lord says of the need to teach students to see interconnections and consider the consequences of their work projects, materials, and breakthroughs.

Drs. Lord and Camacho met at a community engagement event, and realized that they could mine MIDFIELD, a student records database based on partnering multiple universities' information.

"[MIDFIELD] can let us do tremendous quantitative research, but not ask why," Dr. Lord said. So she and Dr. Camacho teamed on several National Science Foundation grants to interview students to obtain the qualitative analysis they needed. An early result was the book *The Borderlands of Education: Latinas in Engineering* (2013).

"It's more about changing engineering than about changing women or people of color," Dr. Lord said. "What we need to fix is our own culture, to be more welcoming and to allow for diversity instead of punishing or penalizing."

That means, in academia, that faculty and staff should seek to listen and understand the students' individual needs in order to respond with appropriate support, advice, and options.

That's true even for subsets of categories, such as women veterans.

Though Dr. Lord said she and Dr. Camacho (2018) studied a sample of 60 students, of whom seven were women who had served in the military, no "one size fits all" model emerged for helping them transition into college. "University faculty and staff could be encouraged to complete trainings or webinars to learn more about student veterans and their assets," their research found. They conducted this research with colleagues Joyce Main, Ph.D., associate professor, Purdue University School of Engineering Education; Catherine Mobley, Ph.D., professor of sociology, Clemson University department of sociology, anthropology, and criminal justice; and Catherine Brawner, Ph.D., president of Research Triangle Educational Consultants.

Dr. Lord's extensive curriculum vitae includes two book chapters, 65 articles published in refereed journals, 139 articles published in conference proceedings, 51 peer-reviewed summaries published in conference proceedings, 94 presentations, guest editorials, magazine articles, tip sheets, and newsletters.

Collaborating with Denise R. Simmons, Ph.D., Dr. Lord offered a relentless critique of engineering culture, demanding that it rise above deeply ingrained exclusionary practices. The title says it all: "Removing Invisible Barriers and Changing Mindsets to Improve and Diversify Pathways in Engineering" (Simmons and Lord 2019). Dr. Simmons is associate professor in the University of Florida department of civil and coastal engineering.

Another collaboration, with Dr. Simmons and Brooke C. Coley, Ph.D., assistant professor in engineering at the Polytechnic School of the Ira A. Fulton Schools of Engineering at Arizona State University, resulted in the publication of "Dissolving the Margins: LEANING INto an Antiracist Review Process" (2021), in the *Journal of Engineering Education*.

One hopeful sign is that Dr. Lord's integrated engineering department won raves from accreditation agency ABET, calling the program "exemplar," "innovative," and "student-centered."

Dr. Lord is leading workshops to show other educators how to teach inclusively, and she sees a possibly more compassionate environment post-COVID.

## YU TAO, PH.D.

"IDEALLY, RECOGNIZING GENDER DISPARITIES IN ENGINEERING AS EMBEDDED IN THE BROADER SOCIETAL AND NATIONAL CONTEXT, ANY ADVANCES THAT WOMEN MAKE — AS A WHOLE AND AS A HIGHLY DIFFERENTIATED GROUP — CAN BENEFIT EVERYONE, LEADING TO GREATER GENDER EQUITY AND BETTER SCIENCE AND ENGINEERING, ENCOMPASSING DIVERSE PERSPECTIVES."

— From: "Gender and Race Intersectional Effects in the U.S. Engineering Workforce: Who Stays? Who Leaves?," Yu Tao, Ph.D., and Connie L. McNeely, Ph.D.

The engineering community — and science and technology as a whole — must delve into its own gender disparities and people's unique experiences of discrimination and oppression to realize diversity's benefits.

At the same time, it's important to recognize that, even among minority women, their interests and outcomes in engineering vary.

For example, Black women have a lower probability than African American men, but a greater probability than White and Latina women to earn a bachelor's degree in electrical and computer engineering.

But Black women are one of the groups with the lowest probability of actually working in electrical and computer engineering jobs among all gender and racial/ethnic groups, according to the research (2021) by **Yu Tao, Ph.D.**, and her co-author, Cheryl Leggon, Ph.D., associate professor in the School of Public Policy at the Georgia Institute of Technology. They wrote their findings in a chapter titled "African American Women in Engineering: Intersectionality as a Pathway to Social Justice." It appeared in the book *Social Justice and Education in the 21st Century: Research from South Africa and the United States*, by Willie Pearson Jr., Ph.D., and Vijay Reddy, Ph.D., Eds. (2021).

Even more intriguing, no gender differences exist in achieving an engineering occupation among African Americans, Asian Americans, and Latinas/Latinos who earned doctorate degrees in engineering. This finding suggests the equalizing

effect of an engineering doctoral degree to men and women.

These findings stem from drill-down research into Black, Latina, Asian, and women engineers who identify as different genders by Dr. Tao, associate professor of sociology at the Stevens Institute of Technology in Hoboken, New Jersey. Dr. Tao earned her Ph.D. in the sociology of science and technology from Georgia Tech and her master's degree in educational media technology from Boston University, the latter in half the program's usual 18-month time frame.

"Ideally, recognizing gender disparities in engineering as embedded in the broader societal and national context, any advances that women make — as a whole and as a highly differentiated group — can benefit everyone, leading to greater gender equity and better science and engineering, encompassing diverse perspectives," according to Dr. Tao's co-authored article (2019) with Connie L. McNeely, Ph.D., a sociologist and professor of public policy at George Mason University, "Gender and Race Intersectional Effects in the U.S. Engineering Workforce: Who Stays? Who Leaves?"

Dr. Tao, who grew up in Shanghai, began researching gender and other inequities in engineering by doing data analysis for her Ph.D. advisor at Georgia Tech, Willie Pearson Jr., Ph.D., a professor of sociology in the School of History and Sociology. Dr. Pearson, whom President Barack Obama appointed to his Board of Advisors on Historically Black Colleges and Universities, has published several books on the experiences of African American scientists with Ph.D.s, including major studies on chemists and engineers.

That led to Dr. Tao's research detailing the many challenges that Black women face in STEM education and in their careers, ranging from being stereotyped to having fewer mentors to getting nowhere in their careers.

Now, Dr. Tao is working to increase interest and retention in the engineering profession among women and other underrepresented groups.

Dr. Tao and Ye Yang, Ph.D., an associate professor in the School of Systems and Enterprises at Stevens Institute of Technology and the principal investigator, will start this summer proposing ways to improve teaching in undergraduate software engineering.

That's because, even as websites crash under the weight of user traffic in the real world, the concept of performance in software development is rarely a topic of classroom discussion.

Dr. Tao and Dr. Yang are designing a toolkit that aims to give software engineering students "real world" examples that address inequality and social justice, in part to show how important performance is to their work. Dr. Tao will evaluate whether the toolkit could also increase retention of women students in software engineering.

Though a more expansive teaching style, including greater student interactivity and studying social and political events, remains rare in engineering higher education, researchers are increasingly leveraging their skill to address such issues as race, class, gender, and ethnicity in housing, transportation, and other policies, Dr. Tao said.

One example is the Data Science for Social Good initiative, which aims to focus data science research to benefit people in the developing world and other marginalized communities.

### PRIVACY RESEARCH AIMS AT DATASET EQUITY

Dr. Tao currently is studying how to equal the playing field in the realm of "fair privacy" — fairly protecting online users' information captured in datasets.

She is doing so along with Hui Wang, Ph.D., principal investigator for the study's National Science Foundation grant, and associate professor of computer science in the School of Engineering and Science at Stevens Institute of Technology.

## A Reverence for Teaching and an Affinity for Technology

Yu Tao, Ph.D., grew up in Shanghai revering her teachers. "I wanted to be a teacher," she said. "They were my role models." That's why Dr. Tao earned an undergraduate degree in English.

Her focus changed while she worked on her thesis — creativity and innovation in technology. She said she was drawn to technology even farther as she delved into magazine and newspaper coverage.

Dr. Tao worked for a tech company as a team assistant and quickly moved into supply chain management. She said she found it fulfilling to "make things work."

"If there's no good supply chain management, nothing would move forward," she said.

But Dr. Tao had higher ambitions, so she moved to the United States in 2003 to study instructional technology. She finished Boston University's 18-month Master of Education program in half that time and spent her final summer there traveling the country with friends.

She said she loved Boston for its cultural attractions, relative quiet compared with New York, and her first experience with snow.

"The first snow was a snowstorm that lasted two days," she said. "That was the most snow I had ever seen."

Dr. Tao moved into the deep data analysis of STEM fields phase of her career — and an entirely different weather world — while she earned her Ph.D. at Georgia Tech in Atlanta.

While all users in online datasets are anonymous, it is actually possible to identify certain users and, based on their backgrounds, some are more easily identified than others, making them more vulnerable to privacy attacks.

That's why it's so important to ensure all users' information is protected equitably, Dr. Tao said. ✿

## References

Atkinson, R., Mobley, C., Brawner, C., Lord, S.M., Camacho, M., and Main J. (2018). I Never Played the "Girl Card": Experiences and Identity Intersections of Women Student Veterans in Engineering. American Society for Engineering Education Annual Conference, Salt Lake City.

Bilimoria, D. and Liang, X. (2015). *Gender Equity in Science and Engineering: Advancing Change in Higher Education.* Routledge Studies in Management, Organizations and Society.

Bilimoria, D. and Stewart, A.J. (2009). "Don't Ask, Don't Tell": The Academic Climate for Lesbian, Gay, Bisexual, and Transgender Faculty in Science and Engineering. *NWSA Journal* 21(2): 85–103.

Camacho, M. and Lord S.M. (2013). *The Borderlands of Education: Latinas in Engineering.* Lexington Books: Lanham, Maryland.

Cech, E. (2013). Ideological Wage Inequalities?: The Technical/Social Dualism and the Gender Wage Gap in Engineering. *Social Forces* 91(4): 1147–1182.

Cech, E. and Blair-Loy, M. (2019). The Changing Career Trajectories of New Parents in STEM. *Proceedings of the National Academy of Sciences.* 116. 201810862. 10.1073/pnas.1810862116.

Cech, E. and Rothwell, W. (2018). LGBTQ Inequality in Engineering Education. *Journal of Engineering Education* 107(4): 583–610.

Cech, E. and Waidzunas, T. (2011). Navigating the Heteronormativity of Engineering: The Experiences of Lesbian, Gay, and Bisexual Students. *Engineering Studies* (3)1: 1–24.

Cech, E. and Waidzunas, T. (2021). Systemic Inequalities for LGBTQ Professionals in STEM. *Science Advances* 7(3).

Cech, E., Waidzunas, T., and Farrell, S. (2016). Engineering Deans' Support for LGBTQ Inclusion. American Society for Engineering Education Annual Conference, New Orleans.

Coley, B.C., Simmons, D.R., and Lord, S.M. (2021). Dissolving the Margins: *LEANING IN*to an Antiracist Review Process. *Journal of Engineering Education* 110(1): 8–14.

Fouad, N.A. and Singh, R. (2011). "Stemming the Tide: Why Women Leave Engineering." University of Wisconsin–Milwaukee.

Simmons, D.R. and Lord, S.M. (2019). Removing Invisible Barriers and Changing Mindsets to Improve and Diversify Pathways in Engineering. *Advances in Engineering Education*, June 2019.

Tao, Y. and Leggon, C. (2021). African American Women in Engineering: Intersectionality as a Pathway to Social Justice. In *Social Justice and Education in the 21st Century: Research from South Africa and the United States*, W. Pearson Jr. and V. Reddy, Eds. Springer International Publishing: 241–272.

Tao, Y. and McNeely C. (2019). Gender and Race Intersectional Effects in the U.S. Engineering Workforce: Who Stays? Who Leaves? *International Journal of Gender, Science and Technology* 11(1): 181–202.

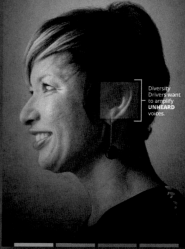

# SWE's Community College Research: Understanding Women's Experiences on the Transfer Pathway

Community colleges play an important role in helping to diversify the engineering and technology professions because many underrepresented groups, specifically women and people of color, begin their educations in these settings.

By Roberta Rincon, Ph.D., SWE Associate Director of Research

Less than half of the undergraduate student population pursues what we often refer to as the "traditional path" to a STEM degree — entrance into a four-year university immediately following high school graduation.[1] There are a variety of alternative pathways available to those seeking a STEM education, such as two-year colleges and the for-profit sector. Increasingly, students are earning college credit from multiple institutions, including those who transfer from a two-year to a four-year institution. Approximately 36% of undergraduate students attend a two-year college, and almost 60% of those students are women.[2] Community college is also a popular pathway for students of color, who are overrepresented among community college student enrollments.[3]

In 2016, SWE began a phased study to understand whether women who started their college studies at a community college with intentions to earn a bachelor's degree in engineering or computer science (ECS) were completing degrees in these fields. SWE wanted to know whether women were transferring to four-year institutions at similar rates to men and earning bachelor's degrees in these majors and, if not, what challenges women faced on the transfer pathway. SWE's study was conducted in three phases, with the final phase concluding in 2021.

## PHASE I: CLARIFYING THE PROBLEM

Research has found that more than 80% of first-time community college students want to complete a bachelor's degree, but only about one-third successfully transfer to a four-year institution, regardless of major.[4,5] Approximately 15% of two-year college students declare a major in ECS, and of those who transfer to complete a bachelor's degree, more than 65% are successful.[6] Consider these figures in light of the diverse student population that begins their studies at a community college, and we can see the potential to increase the number of diverse graduates entering the engineering workforce if we can better support students to and through the transfer process.

Funded by SWE's Corporate Partnership Council, Phase I looked at 10 years of education data housed at the Texas Education Research Center. Texas was selected because of ease of access to student-level transfer data, the diversity of the population, and the fact that the majority of bachelor's degree earners in the state had prior enrollment in a two-year community college — though not necessarily as transfer students.[7] Researchers looked at disaggregated data by gender and race/ethnicity, where possible. In some cases, low student counts for female subpopulations made it difficult to determine the successful transfer and degree completion for women of color, but that itself was an important finding: There are very few women of color who successfully transfer from a community college and complete bachelor's degrees in ECS in Texas.

Some of the major findings from this descriptive analysis of student enrollment, transfer, persistence, and degree completion were:

- **Fewer than 2% of women** who transfer from a two-year college to a four-year university majored in ECS compared with 11% of men.
- **Approximately half of women** who majored in ECS and transferred from a two-year college to a four-year university completed bachelor's degrees in ECS.
- Over 60% of two-year colleges in this study had more than 100 men who transferred and completed a bachelor's degree in ECS, but **only 3%** had more than 100 women transferred and graduated in ECS.
- Regardless of gender, students who begin at a two-year college and declare a major in ECS often switch out of these majors. However, **more women than men switch majors**, with some colleges experiencing more than half of women switching out of ECS majors and completing degrees in other majors.

Across the 10 years of Texas education data that SWE analyzed, fewer than 1,300 women transferred from a two-year college and graduated with a bachelor's degree in ECS compared with almost 9,000 men. This equates to approximately 14% of the total bachelor's degrees earned in ECS by transfer students being earned by women — far fewer than the approximately 21% of total ECS bachelor's degrees earned by women nationally. Acknowledging the limitations of extrapolating the findings from a single state to a national landscape, this study exposed concerning trends on the community college pathway. Considering that women represent more than half of college enrollments, researchers questioned why so few women who start at a community college were completing their bachelor's degrees in ECS.

One of the recommendations from the study was to find out what community college students need to be successful in ECS. What specific challenges and obstacles are women experiencing on this pathway? Are there programs and services that a professional society like SWE could offer to meet their needs? Phase II aimed to answer these questions.

## PHASE II: UNDERSTANDING THE CHALLENGES

For Phase II, SWE collaborated with researchers from the University of Washington's Center for Evaluation and Research for STEM Equity. With funding from SWE's Corporate Partnership Council and the Northrop Grumman Foundation, researchers conducted a mixed-methods study of community college students to investigate the differential rates of persistence in ECS, understand the factors that contribute to their success, and identify challenges that women and other underrepresented students in STEM experience prior to transferring to complete a bachelor's degree. The findings from this research would be useful in determining the types of programs and services that could be developed to support students on the community college pathway in ECS.

The Phase II study comprised a survey of more than 400 community college students in Texas and interviews with community college students and faculty. Survey questions asked about engineering self-efficacy, motivations, and confidence. Interview questions helped researchers identify key supports students received and the barriers they faced on the transfer pathway. Five key recommendations resulted from this research:

- **Improve advising for transfer students:** Students felt uncertain about the help that they received from college advisors, with more than 25% expressing feelings of dissatisfaction with advising on their campuses.
- **Provide more financial support:** It is no surprise that students expressed concern about college costs. While some reported a lack of finances to be a likely reason for them to withdraw from classes or college, others spoke of the impact that working while taking classes had on their ability to make time for academic and extracurricular activities.
- **Provide more information about career pathways:** More than half of students expressed limited or no knowledge about the engineering profession prior to entering college, and women

learned less than men about engineering as a profession during their time at community college.

- **Strengthen interpersonal relationships, networking, and mentorship:** Many students recognized the academic, social, and professional benefits associated with participating in extracurricular activities. While a number of students expressed interest in joining professional societies, few were members of such organizations.
- **Focus on boosting confidence:** Women surveyed expressed less confidence in math and science ability than men, regardless of actual capability. Research suggests that interventions that connect women with same-gender STEM experts can counteract stereotypes and increase their confidence.

The findings from Phase II were extremely enlightening in helping SWE identify ways in which the organization could better support women on the community college pathway. SWE focused on three of the five recommendations — providing information about career pathways, strengthening interpersonal relationships, and boosting confidence — as initiatives that the organization was best equipped to address. This resulted in SWE's creating a pilot networking program to introduce women in community college to STEM professionals, promote relationship building, and increase confidence to encourage them to continue to pursue an ECS degree.

### PHASE III: SWE'S PILOT NETWORKING PROGRAM

In November 2019, SWE obtained funding from the Northrop Grumman Foundation to host six networking sessions for community college women in specific geographic locations in 2020. Then the COVID-19 pandemic hit, and in-person events were postponed. SWE originally intended to push back the in-person events to fall 2020, but the pandemic continued to create an unsafe environment for large gatherings. To prevent further delay, SWE decided to host the networking events online.

Phase III included six virtual networking events, three in spring 2021 and three in fall 2021. The evaluation of this networking intervention involved two main questions:

1. Does the STEM networking intervention increase community college women's motivation, self-efficacy, and confidence in ECS?

## Participants' Comments

- "In my classroom, when it is an introductory course, you see among 20 students, 30 students, it's almost half and half, 50–50, and sometimes the female students are actually dominant compared to the male students at the introductory–level courses. When we get to the advanced courses in computer science, we are lucky if we have two or three female students." – Computer science faculty member at a community college

- "I don't really know anyone else who's doing what I'm doing … I guess it would be nice to be involved in something like [a professional engineering organization] just to hear what other people are interested in or what other people are getting involved in." – Female community college student

### EVENT SURVEY FEEDBACK

- I enjoyed "actually getting to talk to the people. And interacting with the other people in the chat. It isn't normally something that I enjoy, but it was fun at this event."

- I appreciated "getting to hear from someone in my major about hardships and how to keep going."

- "I loved that [Dr. Grayson] shared honestly about how unconventional her journey was. It was encouraging and I was able to see myself in her."

## Figure 1: Survey respondent demographics

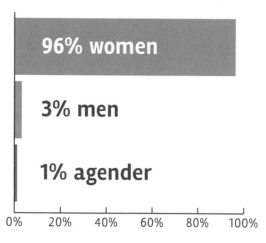

96% women

3% men

1% agender

0%  20%  40%  60%  80%  100%

AVERAGE AGE | MEDIAN AGE
26 | 23

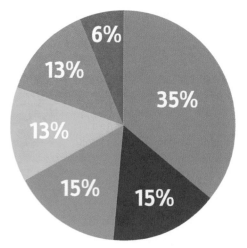

35% White, 15% Asian
15% Middle Eastern/North African
13% Black, 13% Hispanic, 6% Other

2. Does the STEM networking intervention result in greater retention of community college women in engineering and computer science programs?

SWE collaborated once again with researchers from the University of Washington to understand the impact of connecting women in community college to women in four-year university STEM degree programs as women in the STEM workforce. Surveys were sent before each virtual event to those who registered to attend. Immediately after each event, a second survey was sent to those who attended. In addition to the pre-event and post-event surveys, a six-month follow-up survey was sent to those who attended the three spring events. Qualitative data collected included responses from open-ended survey questions and a handful of interviews with students who registered to attend the spring 2021 events.

A total of 132 people attended across the six virtual networking events. This was approximately one-third of those who registered to attend. The events were open to anyone interested, including university students and professionals, though

the focus was primarily on women enrolled in community college. Of those who attended, about 63% provided demographic information. Of these, 56 were undergraduate students, and 18 attended a community college. Figure 1 provides sample demographics of survey respondents.

### Engaging Speaker Series

The spring and fall events followed a relatively similar format, with the first half of the event focused on a presentation or moderated discussion, and the second half providing an opportunity for interaction among those in attendance. However, there were some differences.

In the spring, the three virtual events were presented as a series called "Unleash Your Inner STEM." Each event included a moderated panel discussion followed by small group discussions focused on specific topics of interest and facilitated by a STEM professional. Topics included "Different Types of STEM Careers," "Promoting Your Identity," and "Mentoring." Remo was the platform used to host the events. This platform allowed participants to move around virtual discussion tables and interact with facilitators and other attendees, but it required a separate registration through Remo to attend.

In the fall, the speaker series was called "#Renew. #Relaunch. #Reimagine." SWE moved from a panel discussion to a single guest speaker, giving speakers time to share their stories before opening the floor for questions from the moderator and audience. Instead of Remo, SWE used Zoom to host these events in the hope that a more familiar platform would make students more inclined to attend. After each speaker, Google Jamboard was used to facilitate interaction among the participants. Based on feedback from the fall events, Jamboard was seen as a less intimidating way to encourage interaction. Figure 2 shows an example from one of the Jamboard sessions, where participants were asked to share their thoughts about how women engineers can support other women engineers.

### Evaluating Impact

Due to the small number of survey respondents, it was not possible to draw inferential conclusions. Researchers reported descriptive statistics and reviewed qualitative data to gain insight into how the events were received.

To understand the impact of the networking events on women's motivation, self-efficacy, and confidence, students were asked whether the events were beneficial:

- More than 80% agreed or strongly agreed that the event expanded their understanding of the potential career and educational pathways available to STEM students.
- More than 90% agreed or strongly agreed that the event helped them see themselves as a part of a broader STEM community.
- More than 80% agreed or strongly agreed that they felt more confident in their ability to succeed in their desired career or education pathway.
- Approximately 80% agreed or strongly agreed that they met people in the STEM industry who could be valuable resources for them.

Feedback received on event satisfaction was generally very positive. Participants appreciated hearing from women from diverse backgrounds and professions who were willing to share honestly about their experiences.

Students were asked to rate themselves on specific traits compared with their classmates, including self-confidence, science ability, and communication ability. Researchers compared pre-event and post-event survey responses to gauge

## Figure 2: Sample Jamboard session

## Figure 3: Changes in pre-event versus post-event responses

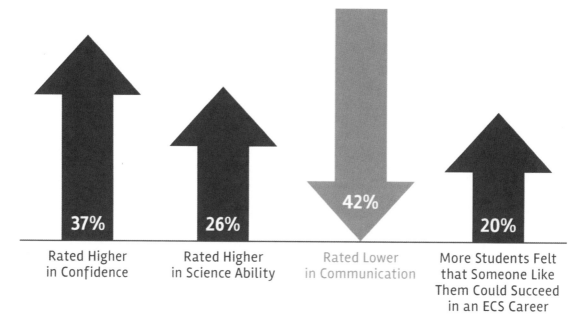

| | | | |
|---|---|---|---|
| **37%** | **26%** | **42%** | **20%** |
| Rated Higher in Confidence | Rated Higher in Science Ability | Rated Lower in Communication | More Students Felt that Someone Like Them Could Succeed in an ECS Career |

whether students' ratings changed. Figure 3 shows some of the observed differences. While 37% of students rated themselves higher in confidence after the event, and 26% rated themselves higher in science ability, students rated themselves lower after the event in terms of communication ability. Qualitative feedback indicated that some students may have been intimidated by the use of the term "networking" when SWE marketed the event. There also seemed to be more interaction among participants in the fall events when the Jamboards were used compared with the spring events, when participants were expected to speak or use the chat function to communicate. The drop in communication ability ratings may also have been influenced by the virtual nature of the events themselves. In-person events may see different results.

The response rate for the six-month follow-up survey was too low to allow for adequate analysis to determine whether the STEM networking events resulted in greater retention of women on the community college pathway in ECS. However, researchers were able to gain some insight into students' expectations for the future when comparing pre-event survey responses against post-event survey responses:

- Students reported more confidence in pursuing a career in ECS after the events than before the events.
- Of those students who responded to both the pre-event and post-event surveys, 20% reported being more likely to pursue a career in ECS after attending the event.

### What's Next

While the switch from in-person to virtual events made them available to a larger audience, it did present significant drawbacks. Virtual networking can be challenging in the best of times, but it can be particularly difficult to market such events to students who are unfamiliar with or intimidated by the act of networking. Marketing these events and encouraging community college students to attend was the most challenging aspect of this project.

One takeaway from Phase III is a greater understanding of the competing priorities that community college students face. Students interviewed who had registered but did not attend noted that they had other commitments, including academic and family responsibilities, that ended up taking precedence over the SWE event.

Another takeaway is the need for SWE to be

more creative when marketing to community college students. A number of people who were interviewed or provided comments on the surveys noted that SWE needed to improve its marketing. Some suggested exploring platforms such as Slack or Discord, while others suggested reaching out to other professional engineering associations when such events are held. While SWE did reach out to its network, sharing the event with other associations and through various communication channels, the reach into the community college space could be improved.

SWE learned a great deal from hosting these networking events. Since launching Phase III, SWE has a new Community Colleges Affinity Group and is working to be more inclusive of women in the two-year college community space. While there are no plans for another community college or transfer study at this time, SWE intends to continue exploring ways to engage students on the transfer pathway and bring them into the SWE network. SWE staff will be connecting with the Community College Affinity Group members to find new, creative, and effective ways of supporting students. In particular, SWE is considering ways in which activities could take place at a more local level to encourage the personal relationships that will best support women who want to transfer to complete their ECS degrees and enter the STEM workforce.

You can read the reports and conference papers that resulted from this phased research study on SWE's Research site at https://swe.org/research/. Recordings of the speakers from each of the six virtual events are available on SWE's Advance Learning Center or on SWE's YouTube channel under the SWE Research playlist. ✿

## Acknowledgments

This research was made possible by the generous support of the Society of Women Engineers' Corporate Partnership Council and the Northrop Grumman Foundation. SWE would like to thank Gibson Consulting for their contributions to Phase I, and Emily Knaphus-Soran, Ph.D.; Erin Carll, Ph.D.; and Alexandra Schaefer from the University of Washington's Center for Evaluation and Research for STEM Equity for collaborating on Phases II and III of this study. This study also benefited from the contributions of SWE staff members Abby Watson and Mary Firor for networking event logistics and University of Texas at Austin doctoral candidate Ursula Nguyen for qualitative data collection and analysis.

Two of the six events, one in the spring and one in the fall, were co-hosted by the Pioneer Valley Women in STEM (PVWIS). Beth McGinnis-Cavanaugh, a professor at Springfield Technical Community College, PVWIS executive board member, and co-chair of SWE's Community Colleges Affinity Group, was instrumental in the planning and delivery of these events. SWE would also like to thank Melissa Paciulli, Ph.D.; Isabel Huff; and Michelle Rame for their help in planning these events.

## Endnotes

1. National Academies of Sciences, Engineering, and Medicine. (2016). *Barriers and Opportunities for 2-Year and 4-Year STEM Degrees: Systemic Change to Support Students' Diverse Pathways.*

2. U.S. Department of Education. National Center for Education Statistics. IPEDS, Fall 2020, 12-Month Enrollment Component (provisional data).

3. Bailey, T. (2012). Can Community Colleges Achieve Ambitious Graduation Goals? In A.P. Kelly and M. Schneider (eds.), *Getting to Graduation: The Completion Agenda in Higher Education* (pp. 73–101). Baltimore: The Johns Hopkins University Press.

4. Horn, L. and Skomsvold, P. (2011). *Community College Student Outcomes: 1994-2009.* National Center for Education Statistics.

5. Jenkins, D. and Fink, J. (2016). *Tracking Transfer: New Measures of Institutional and State Effectiveness in Helping Community College Students Attain Bachelor's Degrees.* Community College Research Center.

6. Chen, X. (2014). *STEM Attrition: College Students' Paths into and out of STEM Fields.* National Center for Education Statistics.

7. National Student Clearinghouse Research Center. (2017). *Snapshot Report: Contributions of Two-Year Public Institutions to Bachelor's Completions at Four-Year Institutions.*

# How Do Young Women Develop an Engineering Identity?

Exploring the views and experiences of young women who are highly committed to engineering may provide insights into best practices to support their aspirations and promote gender equity.

By Catherine Riegle-Crumb, Ph.D., and Ursula Nguyen, The University of Texas at Austin

Despite the extensive body of research dedicated to understanding the factors associated with young women's relatively low levels of engineering interest, there is limited research focusing on young women who have expressed interest in pursuing engineering. Researchers from The University of Texas and the Society of Women Engineers, therefore, have partnered in a longitudinal, mixed-methods project funded by the National Science Foundation (NSF) that focuses on the latter. Broadly, this collaborative research project explores the views and experiences of young women who are highly committed to engineering. The explicit attention on this unique group of young women is intended to understand whether and how young women who have strong inclinations toward engineering maintain their engineering trajectories. Hence, this research project aims to examine the experiences of young women who potentially make up the next generation of women engineers.

To do so, we recruited a diverse sample of young women, including those in high school and college, from across the United States, who are affiliated with SWE. High school students are participants of SWENext, the youth division program of SWE focused on supporting girls in K-12 who are interested in engineering and technology careers. These young women in high school completed online surveys; moreover, members of the research team also conducted in-depth interviews with a select group of high school participants over a period of three years, beginning in the summer of 2019. At the same time, undergraduate women who are SWE collegiate members pursuing engineering

majors were also surveyed each spring, starting in spring 2019. Both surveys and interviews asked participants about themselves, including their STEM attitudes and views about their gender identities, as well as their engineering experiences, such as perceptions of support from others and participation in STEM-related activities.

In this article, we describe three separate studies that come from this larger research project. The first study provides a rich description of both the encouragement and discouragement young women in high school report from multiple actors, including peers and adults. The second study also focuses on SWENext high school participants and investigates their views of gender inequality and their self-efficacy to change inequality in the future. In the last study, we shift our attention to collegiate SWE members and examine their self-perceptions about various dimensions of their gender identities. These studies are grounded in social science theories, which articulate how gender inequality, and gender itself, is socially constructed. Taken together, these studies provide a deeper understanding on the experiences of young women who have articulated a strong engineering interest.

## HOW ARE YOUNG WOMEN ENCOURAGED AND DISCOURAGED?

As mentioned above, this first study explores the inclusionary and exclusionary experiences of young women in high school. In particular, it examines how young women in SWENext are encouraged and, simultaneously, discouraged by various groups of individuals in their lives, including parents, teachers, friends, and classmates. It also investigates whether there is any variation across sources, such that peers may provide more support than adults, or by the gender of the source. For this mixed-methods study, we utilize survey responses from a diverse sample of 133 SWENext young women from across the United States; of these, 33 participated in interviews.

For the quantitative component, we analyzed survey items that asked young women to report the amount of STEM support they receive from peers, teachers, and parents. In general, SWENext young women receive high levels of support. At the same time, they reported more support for their STEM aspirations from adults, including parents and teachers, than from their peers. For example, 89% and 76% indicated strong support from their mothers and fathers, respectively. We also found some evidence of a gendered pattern in the amount of support young women perceived from their peers. For example, they indicated higher levels of support from female friends and classmates than from male friends and classmates, respectively. In other words, SWENext young women viewed boys from their STEM classmates and STEM clubs as providing the least amount of support. For instance, only about 16% of SWENext members reported strong support from male peers.

We turn to qualitative findings from our interviews with young women to describe how they are encouraged and discouraged in their STEM pursuits by these different groups of individuals. As described earlier, young women indicated more support from parents and teachers than from peers. Specifically, they described teachers and parents of any gender as important sources that *push and advocate* for them. This included encouraging young women to take specific actions, such as enrolling in more advanced STEM classes and joining after-school STEM clubs. These adults also demonstrated to young women that they

*recognize and believe in them* as capable of becoming engineers. In doing so, young women felt validated in participating in STEM spaces.

However, young women also discussed being actively discouraged. In particular, they described how they were discouraged from pursuing engineering by boys in their STEM classes and extracurricular activities. This group of young men discouraged SWENext young women through *physical exclusion*, such that boys tended to physically take over materials and spaces. For example, young women expressed how some young men would not allow them to use specific tools and, therefore, limited young women's ability to fully participate and engage in STEM. It is no surprise then that young women indicated lower levels of support from these young men in the survey items, as described earlier in the quantitative results. Along the same lines, young women also pointed out how young men would *take ownership of ideas*, including taking credit for young women's ideas. In doing so, they undermined the work and abilities of SWENext young women.

Stepping back, while on average, young women in SWENext indicated receiving lots of STEM encouragement, their discussion of discouragement from their male peers is concerning. Since boys often constitute the numerical majority in STEM spaces, these discouraging behaviors from young men restrict young women's ability to be recognized as legitimate participants in these spaces, which in turn, can lead to their pushing young women out of engineering before they even enter college. As such, we hope STEM teachers and facilitators of STEM activities become aware of boys' exclusionary behaviors and take action to make STEM spaces more inclusive and supportive of young women.

> WE ALSO FOUND SOME EVIDENCE OF A GENDERED PATTERN IN THE AMOUNT OF SUPPORT YOUNG WOMEN PERCEIVED FROM THEIR PEERS. FOR EXAMPLE, THEY INDICATED HIGHER LEVELS OF SUPPORT FROM FEMALE FRIENDS AND CLASSMATES THAN FROM MALE FRIENDS AND CLASSMATES, RESPECTIVELY.

## HOW DO YOUNG WOMEN THINK ABOUT WOMEN'S UNDERREPRESENTATION IN ENGINEERING?

The second study also focuses on the perspectives of high school young women in SWENext; specifically, it investigates how they understand and make sense of women's underrepresentation in engineering, and how they anticipate dealing with gender inequality in their future careers. This qualitative study draws only from interview data from the first year of data collection (summer 2019), and so, the qualitative sample is composed of the 33 young women from different racial backgrounds who participated in our interviews prior to entering college.

We found that a small percentage of our respondents expressed an *individualistic understanding of gender inequality*, such that they attributed the relative lack of women in engineering to the fact that women "just were not interested" or not aware of opportunities. In contrast, most young women in our sample expressed a *systemic understanding of women's underrepresentation in engineering*, meaning that they were aware of how societal stereotypes about gender shaped people's expectations of what women and men can do, and how such biases are present in individuals and institutions. Such understandings are powerful, as they provide young women with an awareness that many of the obstacles they encounter are not due to their own personal shortcomings. Importantly, we found that Black young women in our study were the most likely to articulate systemic understandings of gender inequality.

Yet when asked to think about their own futures in engineering, many young women, particularly White women, expressed what we refer to as *lean-in self-confidence*, such that they were not worried about entering a male-dominated field rife with gender stereotypes and felt that they could navigate it and be successful. While on the one hand such confidence is positive, on the other hand, it appears that these young women are not very concerned with confronting or trying to dismantle inequality as long as they are personally successful. In contrast, a small group of young women in our study did express *critical self-confidence*, such that they felt empowered to actually change the male-dominated engineering culture by banding together with other women in their futures. Again, we found that such views were most common among Black young women (as well as among Latina young women), pointing to the importance of taking an intersectional approach to exploring the experiences of diverse young women in engineering.

It's possible that young women's views regarding their understandings of women's underrepresentation in engineering (described above) as well as their motivations to challenge gender inequality may shift over time. Given that all interview participants were not yet in college, their engineering experiences during their first few years in college may contribute to their developing more *systemic understandings*, and in turn, these future experiences may shape their motivations to dismantle gender inequality.

## WHAT ARE THE GENDER IDENTITIES OF COLLEGE ENGINEERING WOMEN?

The third study focuses on a different group of young women as it explores how SWE collegiate members view their gender. In general, these young women are distinct from other women in that they have chosen to pursue a male-dominated field. Yet their unique career interests are not necessarily indicative of their perceiving themselves as more masculine or less feminine. Consequently, in this quantitative study, we investigate the gender identities and relationships between different facets of gender identity of approximately 1,000 SWE collegiate women. Specifically, we are interested in examining how this group of young women see their gender as being important to them as well as how similarly they view themselves to women and men their age.

Using survey data from across three years of data collection, we find variation in how much importance SWE collegiate women place on their gender. According to their survey responses, young women majoring in engineering expressed placing a moderate level of importance on their gender. Perhaps for many, entering a male-dominated college major has been the first time that their gender identity has become highly salient. Yet, preliminary findings suggest that this measure of gender identity varies by young women's

SWENext activities, including "Invent it. Build it.," SWE's signature outreach event, introduce and support young women interested in engineering.

intersectional identities, such that among women from high socioeconomic backgrounds, Black and Latina women place lower levels of importance on their gender when compared with their White and Asian peers. As engineering is still a predominantly White and privileged space, women of color pursuing engineering may be contending with the well-documented "double bind" they are in, which could include more instances of racial salience rather than gender salience.

Moreover, young women in SWE also express that they see themselves being similar to both women and men their age. In other words, despite their gender atypical career interests, young women do not see themselves as unfeminine or hyper-masculine. Clearly, these findings debunk preconceived notions that assume young women in engineering would indicate viewing themselves as more masculine because they are pursuing a male-dominated field. Taken together, these findings suggest heterogeneity in engineering women's gender identities, which warrants further exploration into how these gender identities may relate to their future persistence in engineering.

## CONCLUSION AND FUTURE DIRECTIONS

To summarize, we have provided a brief overview of three ongoing studies that come from a larger, longitudinal NSF-funded research project that is a collaboration between SWE and researchers at The University of Texas. Ultimately, these studies address a serious limitation in the literature by centering the experiences of young women who have expressed a strong engineering interest as well as considering them a unique yet heterogeneous group. Specifically, we find some commonalities in their engineering experiences, such as receiv-

ing support from various individuals while also experiencing exclusion from young men in STEM spaces. At the same time, we also find variation in how they view gender and gender inequality, as indicated in the last two studies. Our next steps include examining how these views about support, gender, and gender inequality are related to future engineering outcomes, including engineering persistence and identity, which in itself is a strong predictor of persistence. Thus, findings from these studies will contribute to our understanding on how to support young women's engineering aspirations and advance research on gender equity in STEM education. Moreover, we encourage future work dedicated to further exploring the experiences of young women who have already expressed strong inclinations toward engineering as well as amplifying the voices of young women from minoritized backgrounds. ✿

### Author Bios

*Ursula Nguyen is a doctoral candidate in STEM education at The University of Texas at Austin. She has a B.S. in biomedical engineering from UT Austin. Her research interest on issues of equity in STEM education at the intersection of race/ethnicity and gender stems from her experiences as both an educator of STEM subjects and as a past engineering student. Currently, she is a graduate research assistant for Dr. Riegle-Crumb and a graduate research intern with SWE.*

*Catherine Riegle-Crumb, Ph.D., is Professor of STEM Education and Sociology (by courtesy) at The University of Texas at Austin. As a sociologist of education, her research focuses primarily on the role of social contexts in shaping or disrupting inequality in STEM educational and occupational fields.*

# SWE Research Collaborations with DEI Partners Advance Engineering

Research-based strategies are key to advancing both SWE's mission and diversifying the profession. Collaborating with like-minded organizations, SWE's research staff takes on roles ranging from research lead to supportive partner.

By Roberta Rincon, Ph.D., SWE Associate Director of Research

SWE leverages its research and best practices through many collaborative initiatives with other diversity, equity, and inclusion (DEI) organizations. Often these efforts involve implementing research-based strategies to combat factors that negatively affect women and people of color in science, technology, engineering, and mathematics (STEM). These efforts are critical to SWE's mission and overall commitment to advancing women and those underrepresented within engineering and technology.

SWE members and stakeholders often are uncertain when these programs come up in conversation, thinking, "Yes, I have heard of this project, but I don't know exactly what it entails or SWE's role in the effort."

This article provides an overview of the collaborative activities that involve SWE's research staff, either as a lead or as a supportive partner. The initiatives and resources included are not an exhaustive list of SWE's collaborative efforts, but they are major projects that staff devote time and energy toward achieving our mission to demonstrate the value of diversity and inclusion in engineering and technology.

## SWE AND THE WOMEN OF COLOR IN ENGINEERING COLLABORATIVE

In December 2020, SWE, in collaboration with the National Society of Black Engineers (NSBE) and the Society of Hispanic Professional Engineers (SHPE), received a National Science Foundation grant (NSF Award #2040634) to support the creation of the Women of Color in Engineering Collaborative (WCEC). The purpose of the WCEC is to bring together professional STEM societies and industry partners to address systemic barriers that prohibit equitable work environments for women of color in engineering.

The WCEC includes 28 organizations who are founding partners, working together to create a strategic plan for the collaborative. To date, the WCEC has held two virtual convenings to establish a shared vision and identify the systemic barriers that the WCEC is best positioned to address over the next few years. While the NSF grant ends in June 2022, SWE is working to identify new financing opportunities to support the implementation of the WCEC strategic plan and the growth of the collaborative to include higher education and government partners.

### Why did SWE undertake this project?

Diversity-serving organizations like NSBE, SHPE, and SWE, as well as discipline-specific associations such as the American Society of Civil Engineers, the American Society of Mechanical Engineers, and IEEE, all offer programs and services to support engineers who are under-represented in the profession. Such programs may include affinity groups, DEI committees, and special events aimed at educating members in the ways in which individuals and organizations can combat biases and address inequities. In some cases, programs and/or activities specifically for women of color are offered.

SWE views the WCEC as a vehicle through which professional societies can work with employ-ers in the public and private sectors to connect people, cross divides, and drive systemic change toward the equity we seek in the engineering and technology professions. By working together, we can leverage resources to promote change, while collectively addressing the barriers that lead to the attrition of women of color.

### Where can I learn more?

The WCEC has created a website to share resources from the founding partners at https://www.womenofcolorengineers.org/. Currently a landing page, the website will soon serve as a source of information and a place of community for those seeking resources to support the inclusion of women of color in their organizations. Learn more about the WCEC at womenofcolorengineers.org and be sure to revisit the site as it will be up-dated with more resources.

---

## SWE & ADVOCATES FOR EMPOWERMENT (A4E)

Advocates for Empowerment (A4E) is a gender-parity and equality corporate recognition and benchmarking program offered by SWE. It aims to provide companies actionable information that will help them recruit and retain diverse women in engineering and technology. Scheduled to launch fully later this year, the A4E program is currently in a pilot phase that does not include recognitions. Companies eligible to participate in the program must be for-profit organizations headquartered in the U.S. with at least 150 employees, of which 25 or more are women in engineering positions at each level below executive (senior level, mid level, and professional), and 25 or more are women in tech-nology positions at each level below executive.

The A4E program includes a robust survey that asks eligible companies for data on their top management and engineering and technology workforce; information on programs, policies, and practices to retain and advance diverse talent; and corporate culture. Participating companies that score 70 out of 100 possible points will be recog-nized. Scores are based on the representation of diverse women in the workforce (60 points) and the programs, policies, and practices in place, including employee protections, social responsibility, ac-countability, and transparency (40 points).

In addition to being publicly recognized as best employers for women in engineering and technol-ogy, recognized companies will receive a digital award logo to promote their recognition at SWE's conference and on SWE's Career Center.

### Why did SWE undertake this initiative?

The A4E program uses rigorous methodology to analyze data to provide actionable information and insights to participating companies. SWE will be able to connect outcomes of the top-performing companies to best and promising practices that other companies can use to improve the retention and advancement of diverse talent. Companies that participate year-over-year will be able to see the impact of changes they make to policies and prac-tices on the retention and advancement of diverse engineers. SWE views the A4E program as a "fix the system" solution to address the lack of diversity in the engineering and technology professions.

### Where can I learn more?

Visit SWE's A4E website at https://a4e.swe.org/ to learn more about the program. Companies interested in registering to participate in A4E will have an opportunity to sign up in the spring. For the FY23 cycle, the application will open in July 2022, and company recognitions will be made in early 2023. Find out more by contacting SWE Strategic Partnerships at strategicpartnerships@swe.org.

## SWE AND THE 50K COALITION

SWE, NSBE, SHPE, and the American Indian Science and Engineering Society (AISES) formed the 50K Coalition in 2015. The executive directors/CEOs of AISES, NSBE, SHPE, and SWE serve on the 50K Coalition's Leadership Circle, providing sustained leadership for the coalition to meet its goal. At this time, more than 60 organizations have joined the four founding organizations in their commitment to increase the number of engineering bachelor's degrees awarded annually to students of color and women. The coalition's goal of reaching 50,000 diverse engineering graduates per year by 2025 is a 66% increase over the 2015 benchmark.

The 50K Coalition is a structured collaboration of associations, colleges, universities, agencies, corporations, and foundations working toward a common goal and leveraging their unique missions, relationships, and institutional memories. Using a collective impact framework, the coalition applies an evidence-based approach to drive decision-making, improvements, information sharing, and collective action to reach its goal. The collective impact framework guides the development of a common agenda, the identification of shared metrics, the coordination of reinforcing activities, and continuous communication across the collaborative.

Recent developments have led the 50K Coalition to narrow its immediate focus to two specific areas: undergraduate support and student retention, and community college linkages. These two action

network groups are working to identify activities that support this initiative across the member organizations and collect the data necessary to measure impact, while continuously pursuing funding opportunities and expanding the coalition to include organizations that support the 50K Coalition's common agenda.

### Why did SWE undertake this initiative?

Diversity within the pathway for engineering and technology careers is critical to meeting the global workforce demand. SWE is committed to advancing the profession while reducing barriers for women and others underrepresented within the profession to advance in engineering and technology.

To that end, in early 2015, SWE met with NSBE and SHPE's executive teams to discuss ways that the organizations could work collectively to increase their constituents' representation among engineering undergraduates. They understood that meeting the goal would require commitment from numerous organizations working to increase diversity in the U.S. engineering workforce. With support over the years from the United Engineering Foundation, the National Science Foundation, the Terracon Foundation, and the Clark Foundation, the 50K Coalition Leadership Circle has focused on pulling together a strong coalition of member organizations committed to working together to diversify the engineering profession.

### Where can I learn more?

The 50K Coalition's website at https://50kcoalition.org/ provides information about the initiative, including upcoming and past events, and opportunities to join the coalition.

## SWE AND THE SOCIETIES CONSORTIUM ON SEXUAL HARASSMENT IN STEMM

The Societies Consortium is a member-based organization with a mission "to support academic and professional disciplinary societies in fulfilling their mission-driven roles as standard bearers and standard setters for excellence in science, technology, engineering, mathematics, and medical (STEMM) fields, addressing sexual harassment in all of its forms and intersectionalities." More than 100 STEMM societies are members of the consortium, which is focused on advancing inclusive STEMM conduct, climate, and culture by sharing resources and engaging in community building to promote sustainable change.

Launched in 2019, the Societies Consortium was created by the American Association for the Advancement of Science, the American Geophysical Union, and the Association of American Medical Colleges, working with EducationCounsel as a law and policy expert, in response to the National Academies of Sciences, Engineering, and Medicine's June 2018 Consensus Study Report on sexual harassment in STEMM. The Societies Consortium serves the needs of societies' operations to tackle gender harassment and other forms of discrimination on the basis of sex or gender, with particular attention to the intersectionality of harassment based on race and ethnicity.

### Why did SWE join this initiative?

The Societies Consortium is focused on advancing professional and ethical conduct, climate, and culture in STEMM. This is central to SWE's mission, and while SWE may be one of few participating societies whose membership is not male dominated, there are benefits to SWE's participation in this collective.

As a member of the Societies Consortium, SWE can participate in the creation of an influential and collective voice to set standards of excellence in STEMM fields. SWE provides input into the subject matter, prioritization, and content of the Societies Consortium deliverables, has early access to the resources that the consortium creates, and engages with peers and experts while building a community to drive the climate and culture changes in STEMM that are needed to create more diverse and inclusive STEMM workplaces. To date, the Societies Consortium has created model policies for societies to customize and adopt for meetings conduct, honors and awards, and ethical and professional conduct.

### Where can I learn more?

The Societies Consortium website at https://societiesconsortium.com/ contains information about the consortium, upcoming events, and news about the members of the Societies Consortium and the work that the consortium is undertaking.

## SWE AND THE ARC NETWORK (A STEM EQUITY BRAIN TRUST)

The ADVANCE Resource and Coordination (ARC) Network builds on the work of the National Science Foundation's ADVANCE program, which was created in 2001 to foster gender equity by identifying and eliminating organizational barriers that impede the full participation and advancement of women STEM faculty in academic institutions. The ARC Network aims to connect scholars and practitioners committed to equity in STEM to share knowledge from the NSF ADVANCE program grantees. Through the facilitation of shared tools and resources, and the curation and synthesis of knowledge on systemic change and gender equity, the ARC Network works to empower the community with the tools needed to improve the participation, advancement, and inclusion of diverse women in STEM.

The ADVANCE program is discussed extensively in "Women in Engineering: Analyzing 20 Years of Social Science Literature," the centerpiece article in this issue."

The Women in Engineering ProActive Network serves as the backbone organization for the ARC Network. The ARC Network includes two components: the ARC Network Research and the ARC Network Community. ARC Network Research includes two major programs: the Virtual Visiting Scholars and the Emerging Research Workshops. Both aim to synthesize existing research, produce new research agendas, and provide evidence-based recommendations for policy and practice. The ARC Network Community provides opportunities to connect through news and events, including reports and webinars to share the research outcomes from ARC Network Research activities. The ARC Network also houses a Mendeley resource library, a curated selection of resources to aid the ARC Network Community in their STEM equity efforts. The library includes numerous reports, white papers, toolkits, training videos, and datasets, as well as SWE's annual literature reviews and relevant reports.

## What is SWE's role in this initiative?

SWE is represented on both the research advisory board and the communities of practice committee. These bodies work to select the virtual visiting Scholars and plan the community conven-ings. SWE has participated in ARC Network events as a presenter to share relevant SWE research with the community and provides resources for the Mendeley resource library.

## Where can I learn more?

Learn more about the ARC Network at https://www.equityinstem.org/. The site also provides access to the Mendeley resource library, a valuable resource for those interested in STEM equity research. The website includes articles and webinars highlighting the work of the virtual visiting scholars and reports from the convenings of scholars during the Emerging Research Workshops. ✿

---

While our collaborative efforts are vital to reaching our strategic goals, SWE also works to curate data and research from external sources to share with our members and the public. SWE's research website contains a wealth of information for those seeking data on the landscape for girls and women in engineering and technology, and STEM broadly. All the research activities that SWE undertakes require expertise from both inside and outside the organization. The SWE Research Advisory Council serves as an important resource for staff in determining what projects to undertake, which researchers could serve as strong collaborators, and how best we can share our research outcomes with multiple stakeholder groups.

### SWE RESEARCH SITE

In 2016, SWE launched its research microsite to serve as a one-stop shop for members and the public to find the latest data and information on issues involving girls and women in engineering. The site includes statistics for K–12 education, higher education, and the workplace on topics ranging from intentions to major in engineering to retention of women in the engineering workforce. The site also includes data from countries outside of the U.S. in places where SWE has an active membership or great interest, including India, Mexico, and the United Kingdom.

Last year, SWE redesigned the research web pages and moved them under the SWE.org umbrella. This move allows visitors to the SWE.org site to search for research topics from the main site. The new pages are designed to be easier to navigate, allowing us to categorize SWE's own research under the appropriate topics. We can also gather analytics for the research pages, which will be useful as we continue to grow the site to understand which pages are the most popular and in need of more frequent monitoring to ensure that they remain up-to-date.

For those interested in conducting research with SWE, either in collaboration or seeking assistance with study participant recruitment, contact information is available on the site at https://swe.org/research/. SWE evaluates every research request. The application and evaluation process are available on the site.

## SWE RESEARCH ADVISORY COUNCIL

The SWE Research Advisory Council (RAC) was established in 2018 to help guide and inform the research activities of the organization. In addition to helping to identify research topics for exploration, the RAC helps SWE identify potential collaborators and external funding opportunities, provides expert feedback on current research projects, and supports our efforts to disseminate research findings.

Unlike other committees within SWE, membership on the RAC is by invitation only. The RAC currently has 10 members, providing representation to the council from industry, academia, and the nonprofit sector. Individuals on the RAC include representatives from within and outside the U.S. SWE benefits from the diverse expertise of the members serving on the council.

The current members of the SWE Research Advisory Council are:

- Stephanie G. Adams, Ph.D., dean, Erik Jonsson School of Engineering and Computer Science, The University of Texas at Dallas

- Carlotta M. Arthur, Ph.D., executive director, Division of Behavioral and Social Sciences and Education, National Academies of Sciences, Engineering, and Medicine

- Caterina Cocchi, Ph.D., professor, physics, University of Oldenburg

- Diane Foley, senior director, information technology, Raytheon Co.

- Gretchen Hein, Ph.D., senior lecturer, engineering fundamentals, Michigan Technological University

- Karen J. Horton, P.E., professor, mechanical engineering technology, The University of Maine

- Peter F. Meiksins, Ph.D., Professor Emeritus of Sociology, Cleveland State University

- Andresse St. Rose, Ed.D., director of educational research and evaluation, Education Development Center

- Bevlee A. Watford, Ph.D., P.E., professor, engineering education, Virginia Tech

- Rishelle Wimmer, senior lecturer, information technology and systems management, Salzburg University of Applied Sciences

- Roberta Rincon, Ph.D., associate director of research, Society of Women Engineers

- Anne Perusek, director of editorial and publications, Society of Women Engineers

The RAC currently meets three times each year. SWE is grateful for the time and commitment that our RAC members give to support our research efforts.

# Reviving the Equal Rights Amendment

The Equal Rights Amendment has existed nearly 100 years but is yet to become law. Efforts are underway to change that, invigorated by the state of Virginia's 2020 vote to ratify the ERA and the work of advocates.

By Sandra Guy, SWE Contributor

We've witnessed celebrities and billionaires rocket into suborbital space. We've survived one of world history's deadliest viruses. And NASA engineers launched a space telescope that can see distant planets in far-off galaxies.

But the U.S. Constitution fails to prohibit discrimination on the basis of sex.

Why? It's complicated.

The Equal Rights Amendment (ERA) would prohibit discrimination on the basis of sex — and not just for women. A U.S. Supreme Court ruling on June 15, 2020 extended the protection to people regardless of their sexual orientation and gender identity, said Carol Jenkins, president and CEO of the ERA Coalition and the Fund for Women's Equality, sister organizations dedicated to the ERA's adoption.

"For many years, we described it as 'let's put women in the Constitution,'" Jenkins said.

Jenkins said she now sees the ERA as more expansive — as applying to sex and gender identity — after the Supreme Court's Bostock v. Clayton County ruling, which held that Title VII of the Civil Rights Act of 1964 protects employees against discrimination because they are gay or transgender.

The Equal Rights Amendment's magnitude isn't the only uncertainty.

Amendments to the U.S. Constitution become law when they're ratified by at least three-fourths of U.S. state legislatures — or 38 out of 50.

On Jan. 15, 2020, Virginia became the 38th state to ratify the ERA after its Senate and House of Delegates voted to approve the constitutional change.

Seems simple enough. Not so fast. Turns out that the ERA's preamble included a deadline — the result of a long-ago political compromise — that expired on June 30, 1982, nearly 40 years ago. The deadline itself is a source of contention, since some argue it's unconstitutional.

After Virginia's ERA passage, the nation's archivist, David Ferriero, a 2009 appointee of former President Barack Obama, declined to certify the amendment even though he had previously expressed his support for the ERA. That's because the U.S. Justice Department's Office of Legal Counsel under former President Donald J. Trump issued a memo forbidding Ferriero from publishing it.

Ferriero has announced that he's retiring in April, and the U.S. Senate — *just the Senate, not the U.S. House* — must approve whomever President Biden nominates as Ferriero's replacement.

ERA supporters are urging Ferriero to publish the amendment before he retires.

But on Feb. 8 [2022], three Republican senators — Rob Portman of Ohio, Ron Johnson of Wisconsin, and Mitt Romney of Utah — wrote to Ferriero, seeking his "reassurance" that he won't act on the ERA "until it has been properly ratified and legal questions regarding such ratification have been resolved."

Two efforts are now underway to finally get the ERA included in the U.S. Constitution:

- ERA supporters have proposed legislation in both the U.S. House and the U.S. Senate to remove the deadline to ratify the Equal Rights Amendment — even though legal challenges would be inevitable and despite a federal judge's

Kimberly A. Hamlin, Ph.D., the James and Beth Lewis Professor of History at Miami University in Oxford, Ohio

ERA Coalition CEO and President Carol Jenkins

ruling that the time has already run out for such a change.

- Some Democrats want to insist, as a requirement of confirming Biden's nominee, that the next archivist commit to publishing the ERA.

## ADDITIONAL CONSIDERATIONS

There's another wrinkle that reflects the nationwide debate over abortion rights. The U.S. Supreme Court will decide by this summer whether to overturn or undercut Roe v. Wade, the case that has guaranteed the right to an abortion since 1973.

"The central issue that's animating debate [over the Equal Rights Amendment] is abortion rights," said Kimberly A. Hamlin, Ph.D., the James and Beth Lewis Professor of History at Miami University in Oxford, Ohio. "That's what has gotten ERA opponents motivated, especially now with the potential overturning of Roe v. Wade happening this summer."

Dr. Hamlin said that women could, presumably, depend on an Equal Rights Amendment — if and when it's certified as part of the U.S. Constitution — to demand full-scale reproductive health care.

An ERA in the U.S. Constitution could be interpreted to say that women's equality rests, in part, on access to full-scale reproductive health care and that women's rights must not be subsumed by those of unborn fetuses, Dr. Hamlin said.

"We [historians] look at the ERA as a living, breathing document over 100 years," Dr. Hamlin

said. "When Alice Paul first wrote it in 1923 and revised it in the 1940s, never could she have imagined our evolving perception of sex difference and gender, basically bestowing equal rights on everyone beyond a binary framework."

Indeed, the ERA's history goes back nearly a century — to 1923 — when members of the National Woman's Party turned its attention to women's equality after they had successfully lobbied for women's right to vote.

The U.S. Senate first passed the ERA 49 years later — on March 22, 1972 — and sent it to the states for ratification.

So what can be done?

Jenkins said the ERA Coalition is working to "put more bite" into state and federal laws with the goal of further undergirding equality in several ways.

That means working for stricter equal pay legislation and starting a corporate equality roundtable aimed at creating a universal code of equality in private employment.

It's all about changing existing laws and revising a document that was flawed from the start, Jenkins said.

"As I always say," she said, "the source of this sexism, racism, and misogyny lies in the Constitution itself, the founding document, which left out the indigenous, enslaved people and women — anyone thought not to be a full human being at that time." ✿

# Two Decades of Interesting and Timely Research

Rachel Morford

Karen Horting, CAE

As we do every year, SWE has taken on the enormous task of summarizing broad-ranging, interesting, and timely research about women in engineering. With 20 years of literature reviews behind us, this year we have taken a retrospective view of the last two decades to compile a unique collection of information and analysis, incorporating some of the most relevant research from 2021 into the discussion.

Our retrospective includes a breakdown of what we have learned and what progress has been made to increase the representation of women in engineering, both in academia and industry; areas of consensus in the research along with the areas of dissent. One sidebar of note shows the progress that has been made in academic leadership. In 2001, there were fewer than 15 women serving as deans of engineering. In 2021, that number had increased to nearly 80! Could the National Science Foundation (NSF) ADVANCE program, which has made such a positive impact for women in academia, be a model for moving the needle in industry?

This issue also includes interviews with six researchers whose work has made a significant impact on the women in engineering research

OUR RETROSPECTIVE INCLUDES A BREAKDOWN OF WHAT WE HAVE LEARNED AND WHAT PROGRESS HAS BEEN MADE TO INCREASE THE REPRESENTATION OF WOMEN IN ENGINEERING, BOTH IN ACADEMIA AND INDUSTRY; AREAS OF CONSENSUS IN THE RESEARCH ALONG WITH THE AREAS OF DISSENT.

arena over the past 20 years. Focusing on a variety of research interests within various academic fields, they reflect upon their work, personal backgrounds, and motivations.

We take a final look at students in community colleges moving into four-year engineering curricula. Phase I of this study was completed and discussed in the 2018 literature review. Phase II, completed in 2019, offers a compelling look at why this pathway toward an engineering degree has the potential to increase diversity in the engineering workforce. Phase III focused on the impact of networking to support women making the transition to a four-year institution. The onset of the pandemic forced the networking to move to a virtual platform, making it difficult to build engagement. Still, the study's conclusions provide insight into how professional associations like SWE can make a positive impact on women studying at community colleges. We thank the Northrop Grumman Foundation for their generous support of this work.

## SHAPING THE FUTURE

The issue provides a glimpse of the preliminary results from "Next Generation Engineers: Examining the Pathways of Adolescent Females in SWENext." This study was funded by the NSF (NSF Award #2040634) and conducted in collaboration with The University of Texas at Austin. The study examined the gender identities of SWENext members, to shed light

IN 2001, THERE WERE FEWER THAN 15 WOMEN SERVING AS DEANS OF ENGINEERING. IN 2021, THAT NUMBER HAD INCREASED TO NEARLY 80!

on how these young women view their own gender and make sense of prevailing gender norms and roles. Second, it examined whether and how peers and adults provide support and encouragement for SWENext members' interest in engineering. Lastly, the study examined how these factors help shape girls' decisions to declare an engineering major in college, as well as their engineering-related self-efficacy and identity.

The articles highlighted here represent only a portion of this publication overall. We encourage you to become familiar with the wealth of information contained herein. Our State of Women in Engineering issue is an important tool on the path of fulfilling the SWE mission and achieving a diverse engineering workforce. We hope you find the information compelling and useful.

*Rachel Morford*
*FY22 SWE President*

*Karen Horting, CAE*
*Executive Director and CEO*

Made in the USA
Middletown, DE
04 April 2022